Secret Genealogy II
The Jewish Roots of Our Christian Ancestors
by
Suellen Ocean

Secret Genealogy II
The Jewish Roots of Our Christian Ancestors

by
Suellen Ocean

Published by:
Ocean-Hose
P.O. Box 115
Grass Valley, CA 95945
www.oceanhose.com

Also by Suellen Ocean:
Secret Genealogy
Secret Genealogy III
The Lies of the Lion
The Celtic Prince
The Guild
Gold River
Gone North
Acorns and Eat'em
Poor Jonny's Cookbook

Table of Contents

Secret Genealogy II
The Jewish Roots of Our Christian Ancestors
by
Suellen Ocean

If you are not familiar with any of the words in this book, please take advantage of the glossary in the back. It will make your reading more enjoyable.

The *Ancients* taught their children to love others. My thanks go out to those who love and appreciate those who are different from themselves. And thanks to those of you who share your ancestral findings on genealogical websites, especially those who are open-minded and candid about family. I want to thank my family for having faith and patience and for loving me even though I'm into odd endeavors. We give our loved ones a great gift by letting them be themselves. I hope we can do the same for these ancestors.

Foreword

Welcome to a surreal world of genealogy and vivid history. I am neither an ethnologist nor a linguist. I am an amateur genealogist with a fruitful imagination. Without ancestral speculation, hunches, vibes, intuition and sharing "what if's," we would never uncover the truth of our ancestors. When using *outside the box* thinking and *brainstorming* one does not laugh or ridicule spontaneous ideas as the most unlikely thoughts lead to important discoveries and breakthroughs.

I have had a great response to my book, *Secret Genealogy,* which arose through research I was doing for my historical novels, "*The Celtic Prince*" and "*The Lies of the Lion.*" When I began the research for another novel, "*The Guild"* I knew that I would be compiling my findings into another book and here it is.

A little definition is required before you begin. The Jews originally descended from the holy land but there are several different groups including the Sephardic Jews whose later origins were from North Africa, Spain, Portugal and the Middle East. The Mizrahi Jews are from Babylon and Persia and the Ashkenazi Jews are from Germany, Poland or other areas of Europe. These are not precise definitions. Toward the end of the book I've included a glossary. You may wish to acquaint yourself with it before you read the chapters.

During ancient times there were two sections of the Holy Land: the Northern Kingdom of Israel, which was called Samaria and the Southern Kingdom of Judah, called Judea. Technically, "Jews" are the names of the descendants of Judea but "Jews" is also used when speaking of "Israelites." The twelve tribes of Israel are all the descendants of "Jacob," whose name later became "Israel." During that era, the ancient Hebrews kept strict records of their descendants.

Where do I come up with this stuff? Old and new history books, 1950's encyclopedias, old dictionaries, old maps, conversations, old cookbooks, genealogical websites, family trees and histories, online dictionaries, online encyclopedias, European tourist guide books, the Bible and early ancient "corporate" records. I have conversations with others and analyze the names, dates, facts, figures, historical figures and oral history of their ancestors and of course I study my own family tree.

Old dictionaries are invaluable. Mine has words that have been omitted from modern editions. I use it constantly. It has:
A Pronouncing Gazetteer
More Than Three Thousand Names of Noteworthy Persons
Common English Christian Names (many of them Hebrew)

I also have an old encyclopedia set and I use Internet search engines for researching. I suggest you spend days typing in your surnames into your favorite search engine. Type "Jewish" in front of it and comb through the results looking for clues. The Bible I use has an index and concordance I use to look up a variety of subjects, including first and last names. Even if the names are only vaguely similar there may be an association. The index will lead you to stories in the Bible. That's always fun. You may ask yourself, *is this a connection to my ancestor? Is this a clue?*

If you can't take a few leaps, you are not ready to begin this quest. At first your clues seem outrageous. "No, it can't be. No, no, no," you say to yourself while shaking your head. You confide in friends and family and they think you're a little out there. The lure to find out who your ancestors were is very magnetic. It is as if the ancestors beckon you from the "other world."

Chapter One

In the Beginning

Dr. Albright, the Spence Professor of Semitic Languages at John Hopkins University "frankly told his fellow townsmen of the very close connection in practices, ideas, and even in the turns of a phrase between the people of the Scrolls, the Essenes, and the early Christians, and that the background of the New Testament *is far more Jewish than anyone had ever guessed in print, let alone proved.*"

The Lost Years of Jesus Revealed by Rev. Dr. Charles Francis Potter

I always thought of the Bible as a Christian book about the Christians and Jews and assumed that the Jews had another separate book. But both Christians and Jews use the word Bible. (See glossary: *Torah, Pentateuch*). The Bible has taken on a strong Christian image due to generations of "Bible study groups." There are plenty of non-Christians who live in the southern and mid-United States but the word "Bible belt" has been used for years to define that area. The Bible is Jewish too and to know that helps one to understand the true meaning of Judean-Christianity. The Jews and the Christians are so closely united, if one were to use the analogy of a fruit tree, Judaism would be the rootstock to which Christianity is grafted upon. In fact, even today, the University of Houston undergraduate director of World Cultures & Literature Program, Marie-Theresa Hernandez, is *"working on a project about Crypto-Jews at the highest levels of the church in colonial Mexico."* I believe the analogy of the fruit tree is also quite often the case in family trees.

The Jews never use the term *Old Testament,* that's a Christian term. Judaism has the *Tanakh,* which consists of the same books as in the Old Testament, although the books are not in the same order.

The *Torah* consists of *the five books of Moses* and is one of the books that are included in the *Tanakh*.

In America where we have complete religious freedom, I see and hear evidence of Jews being very careful not to proselytize. Throughout history Jews were persecuted for trying to convert others or for "flaunting" their Jewishness, yet we see Christian missionaries and evangelists doing it all the time.

Christian children are taught in Sunday school to appreciate the geography of the Holy Land but why do we not see a church and synagogue with a big door between them that you can walk through, just as you can go back and forth between the old and new testaments of the Bible? I was taught about the Holy Land and the Old Testament but do not remember being instructed on the rudiments of Judaism. I can tell by the blank stares coupled with silence that most of the people I speak with don't either. Nor does it appear that my parents knew much about Judaism. Fascinating, since they both have Jewish ancestry in their background. I don't believe either of my parents knew of this, especially my mother although my father may have had a hunch.

Lately I was surprised to run across a term I'd never heard before, "Hebrew-Christians." This is an old term appearing in historic census records from the Holy Land and Poland, referring to Jews who considered their ethnicity as Jewish but their religion to be Christian. Of course the earliest Christians were Jews, Christianity began with a small sect of Jews following Jesus, whom we know was also a Jew. I do not know how far back the term "Hebrew-Christian" was used. Undoubtedly there were "Hebrew-Christians" who dropped the Hebrew part of the expression and eventually were known only as "Christian," this is why it is often so difficult for people to accept that their ancestors were Jewish. They had just never heard it said. Historical records of persecution give grand evidence for the reason why the "Hebrew" portion of the expression was dropped.

When I see the word *Jehudi* it makes me wonder if George Lucas didn't borrow a little from the Old Testament. Jehudi is an ancient Hebrew word for Jew. The word "Jew" is sort of an English "nickname," used to designate a man from the Kingdom of Judah (or Judea). The true meaning of a Jew is "a follower of Judaism." This means that one does not have to be born of Jewish ethnicity to be considered a Jew, although the meaning of Jew also means one who is of Jewish ancestry through the matriarchal line. If one's mother is not of Jewish ethnicity one is not considered a Jew unless of course they are a follower of Judaism.

And since I'm mentioning popular movies, do you ever wonder what the Ark of the Covenant was? One, it is a sacred wooden chest. Two, it was made by the tribes of Israel a long, long time ago, well before Christianity. Three, the Israelites made it because the Lord told Moses to tell them to make it. Four, it contained the law (the ten commandments). Five, it was kept in the first temple and was very holy. Six, it was so holy the story is, it caused the River Jordan to divide when they approached with it (remember the Israelites were nomadic for a while so they carried it around). Seven, it symbolized the faith of the Jews. Eight, it was last seen in the Temple in Jerusalem. Nine, it is now a conspiracy theory and Steven Spielberg made a movie about it, *Indiana Jones and the Raiders of the Lost Ark*. Ten, the ancient Babylonians (approx where Iraq is now) burned the Temple down so the Ark must have burned up with the temple. But ... eleven, some religious Jews believe that when the Messiah comes it will be restored.

My ancestors were very religious and saw frugality as a virtue. So when I read about the Essenes, a "splinter Jewish sect," written about in *The Lost Years of Jesus Revealed* by Rev. Dr. Charles Francis Potter, I couldn't help but smile. History doesn't just repeat itself; it keeps continuity, especially in regards to religion.

.".. Essenian in their renunciation of money, in frugality of living, their combining of plain living and high thinking, their mysticism, their interest in hymns and hymn composition, their

3

sunrise worship, their repudiation of animal sacrifices, their asceticism, their connection with Eastern (Persian or Hindu) mystic contemplation, their basic Judaism, their obvious Gnostic coloring, and their studious love of books."
Sound like anyone you know?

For those who one day discover that their ancestors were Crypto-Jews, it's shocking. It's a mind-blowing experience; one just can't explain the feeling. If you had no previous knowledge that your family was Jewish, it stops you dead in your tracks. What? You say. When? You say. And more importantly, why did they hide it? For those of you asking, "What's a *Crypto-Jew?*" the answer is, *one who practices Judaism in secret while professing another religious faith.* Even today in America, a country founded on religious freedom, there are those who when finding that their ancestors were Crypto-Jews, prefer to keep it cryptic. Why? Because this world, no matter where you live, can be very strange in regards to religion.

One of the definitions of religion is *"an awareness or conviction of the existence of a supreme being, arousing reverence, love, gratitude, the will to obey and serve, and the like."* And we have to hide that? Not a good idea to hide it. But religion causes a lot of problems. People have been going to war over it for thousands of years. I guess because each religion becomes such a large umbrella, horrible things often take shelter under that umbrella. Maybe more "live and let live" attitudes and kindness toward one another will help keep the gremlins out from underneath our umbrellas.

Throughout history, houses of worship provide many benefits for their communities. They also provide a treasure trove for genealogists. I find historical houses of worship so interesting, I could design a vacation around them. They leave clues in their architecture, their stained glass windows, their name, their cemeteries nearby, their location, their founders and the year erected. In Indiana, I found a beautiful antique Star of David, stained glass Gothic window embedded in an old Catholic church. I've also heard that there are tiny (microscopic) Stars of David etched into at least one of the stained glass windows of one of Spain's historical Catholic Churches, a sort of rebellious graffiti from the artisans who professed to be *New Christians* but held fast to their Jewish traditions.

Unfortunately, when families change religions *and* surnames to fit within their new surroundings, descendents are left without much heritage. Today, there are resources available for us to explore our "maybe" Jewish roots and it is quite fulfilling.

Nova had a documentary about the lost tribes of Israel and said "This king has been identified with the last king of Israel, Hoshea, who died around the same time, at the time of the Assyrian exile of the ten tribes from Israel." Hosea is a first name that appears in my father's family. Why would my family name their son Hosea, after the last king of Israel if they weren't Jewish? Maybe as Southern Baptists they loved the story, or loved the name but if you are looking at a family tree and trying to decipher it, think of the analogy of a fruit tree. If there is one apple under the tree maybe the apple rolled from an apple tree nearby. But if there are lots of apples under this tree, after awhile you come to the conclusion that indeed it is an apple tree. And related to Hosea, the first known king of Japan was named Osee who ruled around 730 BC. I've read extensive theories of the Jews migrating to Japan thousands of years ago. The similarities are quite convincing.

While helping someone research non-Jewish ancestry in Cleveland, Ohio, I found it interesting that there was an old synagogue in their ancestor's neighborhood. Funny how comfortable some of these "non-Jews" feel living in, or next to, Jewish neighborhoods. Someone could write a book on that topic alone.

Hellenists were a small group of Jews who appreciated Greek culture. They began Christianity. Of course, Jesus was a Jew as was Moses and Noah. Jews fought in the Roman Legions and

5

formed secret societies to aid and comfort one another, as well as offer support to each other's families. They traveled to all the continents, leaving evidence of their pride as Jews, carving those small stars of David into Inquisitional Spanish stained glass church windows and upon Egypt's pyramids. They were a tenacious group, who though having gone cryptic, never gave up the fight. And they left a trail. They left an illuminated pathway leading back to King David's Jerusalem, King Solomon's Temple, the Exile to Babylonia and their scattering (Diaspora) into Europe and the New World. It is with amazement that I follow clues and each day uncover some new revelation marveling at their strength and spirit. But alas, many were emotionally and physically beaten down. In Spain and Portugal history tells of Jewish fathers who killed themselves and their sons before they would succumb to the forced baptisms of the strong arm of the Pope. Jews were forced into arenas by the tens of thousands and all at once sprayed with Catholic baptismal waters. Horrified families fled again and again from a nightmare that followed them wherever they went.

For today's Jews, new technology is enabling the collection of family histories and family trees to be connected, forming a web that spans thousands of years across many continents. You may have adapted the physical characteristics of the geographical area your ancestors finally settled in so you may not think you look "Middle Eastern." Looks are deceiving but the clues and connecting histories are not. If you are reading this book, you have found a clue that is eating away at you.

Chapter Two

Names, Names, Names

It's all about names! Names we find on our family trees, names in the Bible, names of ancient cities that our ancestors were named after, names in other languages that sound similar, names, names, names. You'll notice Americans did funny things with their surnames, creating difficulties for descendants to trace them back to the old country. There was a lot of Anglicizing of names, both first and last. You will be surprised when you start listening and seeing the names through a better wisdom. Early Jewish Immigrants hid who they were because Inquisitional stories were still quite fresh and they wanted to begin new lives partaking of the same opportunities available to other Colonists.

We should not assume that our ancestors three or four hundred years ago were Christians. Yes, they may have their names in church records, Christian marriage records, etc. but this does not mean they were not Jewish. Nor am I trying to say they weren't Christians. They could easily have been Jewish and were either hiding it or in the process of converting. There are many Old Testament names resting upon the graves of our Christian ancestors. If you can't find any ancestry past that headstone, you should try looking at it from another angle.

Sometimes we are traveling down the wrong genealogical trail but when we get on the right road, voila, there it is right in front of us. You aren't going to get anywhere if your ancestors were Jewish and you aren't thinking in that vein. It requires a new mindset, which can be difficult, but Christians find Jewish ancestors – all the time. And they are fortunate when they do. Who wouldn't love to know the names and folklore surrounding our loved ones of long ago, whom without we would not be here?

There's a lot of hoopla these days about whether the new Royal Couple, William & Kate, are Jewish. What's the big deal? It is the hardy rootstock of many a family. Why not embrace it? Kate's mother is a Goldsmith and one author has found a source who believes Princess Diana's mother was a Rothschild and other genealogists insist that Prince William is of the Davidic branch of Jews. How many David's do you know? Are they Davidic? Perhaps not but just as that apple tree gives forth a delightful variety on it's grafted limbs, so our ancient Semitic ancestry provided us with genetic material with which we were free to procreate with other peoples of the world. Be fruitful and multiply the Bible told them. And they did.

And in matters of ancestral oral history, no matter how many years go by, there are those who hold fast and for that we are grateful. Though some will say Afghanistan takes its origins from the Persian word for highlander, there are those who hold fast to oral tradition and insist that it derives from their ancestral line through *Afghana*, the grandson of King Saul, the first *King of Israel*. Bani-Israel (which has various spellings) means "Children of Israel." You may wish to explore your own family origins if you have the surname, Bonte, Banta, Bonnie, etc. as it may have originated as Bani-Israel and your ancestors did not want it to ever be forgotten.

Semitic "defines members of the Semitic language family: the peoples who, in about 3,000 BC, pushed northwards from the Arabian peninsula into Palestine, Syria and Mesopotamia, and down the African continent as far as Ethiopia. Thus, Arabs are as much Semites as Jews."
Johannes Lehmann, *The Hittites, People of a Thousand Gods*

And the same author, Johannes Lehmann, as mentioned above, also points out a rather interesting origin for the name "Cornelius." That name almost deterred me from following this path to uncover Jewish ancestry. "Cornelius" sounds so British, and having a prominent ancestor with that name gave me doubts but I plunged in anyway and Lehmann has given me a new clue when he says, "The fact that Koren tended to be construed as horn, albeit at a later stage, is attributable to the Latin word for horn, the

Semitic-based cornu, from which the name Cornelius, or 'little horn', was formed."

Never underestimate the transformations that names went through - some of them went through a grinder and what came out at the other end did not much resemble the original version. In some instances, there was no original version, only a first time adaptation of the name of the father. And after the death of one who left behind an inheritance, sometimes taking the surname was required to take possession of the estate. That would easily throw off a genealogist.

Ancient Greeks, Jews and Mohammedans did not have surnames. The Jews along with the Welsh began using surnames long after the middle ages. Land-owning Europeans and those of nobility which could have included Jews, took up the practice of maintaining the name of the male line, *surname*, during the 1100s. Though not surnames, these cultures had the following that resembled surnames: the Romans had *Cognomina*, Celts had *clan names* and the Teutonic tribes had *patronymic practices* of adding "ing" as well as Anglo-Saxon tribal name examples such as Harding and Manning.

The use of multiple names is a Hebrew tradition. Hebrew names were used for legal contracts and Ashkenazic Jews blended common German names with Hebrew names.
Sephardic naming patterns differed from Ashkenazic. The Sephardim tended to name their children after living relatives, (first son named after the paternal grandfather, second son named after the maternal grandfather, first daughter named after the paternal grandmother, second daughter named after the maternal grandmother). Children born later were named after the paternal uncle or aunt and then the maternal uncle or aunt and sometimes

after living siblings. Ashkenazi Jews named their children after deceased relatives. If the mother died during childbirth a female baby received the mother's name, otherwise children were named after close relatives who had passed away.

Simon Bening, 1525-30

Since Judah is the name of the ancient kingdom in southern Palestine and he was the son of Jacob, having the surname Jacobsen, Jacob, Jacobi, etc. throughout the centuries is a way of preserving *Jewish identity* though it does not necessarily mean it is always a Jewish name.

When I'm researching a geographical area or family line and come across the coat of arms, if I see swords and helmets, I think, "Well, maybe not" but when I see lions I think, "maybe," and I am encouraged that I could be right, as the lion was the symbol for Judah.

Variations of the Lion surname are: Louis, Lewis, Luis, Luiz, Lyon, Leao, Loewe, Luvesc, etc.

As the identity of these ancestors becomes apparent, why is it that the mere mention of it on the genealogical message boards often brings dead silence and sometimes hostility? What's wrong with being a Jew? Early American Jews were highly moral, hard-working virtuous families having all the qualities that Americans strive for and admire. In fact, my research has brought me to the revelation that these "silent Jews" helped form the basis for what we've often thought was the "Protestant work ethic" or "Christian values." An investigation into the origins of some of the family names woven deeply into the fabric of early American history show they were originally Jews.

Sometimes administrators wrote in the margins of old census records. They may have written a "J" for Jewish. I've seen one entry as "Jow" which made me think they intended to signify that person was Jewish. That entry is what prompted me to look up the spelling of Jew in various online dictionaries. If you have a foreign family name you might try putting it or other "Old Testament" names into the foreign language dictionary search bar, names such as Issac, Jacob, David, Hester, etc and see how they are spelled in that language.

Hungarian: Jew - Zsido, Jewish - Zsido
Polish: Jew - Zyd, Jewish - Zydowski
Spanish: Jew - Judio (male), Judia (female)
Portuguese: Jew - Judeu (male), Judia (female)
Dutch: Jew - Jood or Hebreeer
Friesland: Jew - Joad, Jewish - Hebrieusk

I asked a Jewish friend if she had known any Arabs named David. "No," she said, "too much of a king of the Jews name." Good point. There are Christian Arabs but David is not a common name although it is mentioned in a list of masculine Arabic names as Da'ud or Dawud meaning "beloved" or in the naming of a son after the Prophet David whom I assume they mean King David. I can think of five Davids in my immediate extended family, either first or middle names. Most of us know a David. Yes, it is a common name and who knows how many Davids were named because it was a beautiful name? But who knows how many Davids were named because it was a continued pattern, whether conscious or not to retain *Jewish identity*? Similar sounding surnames David, Davidson, Dovid, Davids, Davi, Davis, Daves, Davin, Davins, Davala, Daviu, Davies, Daud, Daud Ibn, Davila, Davilla and Davision. One French ancestor of mine is "David des Marets." Marets sounds and looks like "Marais" (swamp), the name of the old Jewish Quarter on the Left Bank in Paris. And similar to Marais is Lake Mariout, also spelled Maryut or Mariut, near Alexandria Egypt where there was an ancient Essene community on the shores of this lake and an area where thousands of Jews lived. Be open-minded to various spellings and go with the way a name sounds.

Many of the above versions of the David surname were found at the website www.sephardim.com. This is one of my favorite websites. It has an extensive collection of Jewish surnames. Their search engine is really easy to use. It is one of the first places I go when I'm searching for names.

Sue is a common name. Susanna was a beautiful Jewish "exile" who was accused of adultery by two Jewish elders because she refused their sexual propositions. Her story is written in the Book of Daniel because Daniel came to her side and saved her life as the elders had pronounced a death sentence upon her because she rejected their advances.

Those of you who read my book, "Secret Genealogy" are familiar with an ancestor of mine, Epke Jacobs. There is practically a cult surrounding him on the Internet, partly because there is a wonderful portrait of him from the middle ages. His name, Epke, is a strange one. He hailed from the Netherlands and had a hard time deciding what religion he was going to be, even going so far as to have a Catholic priest into his home to baptize his child, this to me was the confused behavior of a Crypto-Jew and all my research continued to confirm my suspicions that he was Jewish. Jacob is an immensely popular Jewish name. BUT, it's also used all over Europe but what did the Epke mean? It's a very rare name. I have found an ancient Greek male name, "EPIKETOS" which means newly acquired. If you look carefully, you will see that four of the letters removed, form the name "Epke," something medieval Jews did frequently to their names. But while researching the German surname "Koebel" I see that its root is in the Hebrew name Yaakov through the Latin version of Jacobus. Some of the ways you'll find the name Jacob written is: Akev, Hupka, Koop, Goacovo, Jacobi,

Jacques, Iacopo, Giacopo, Kubica and Koepke, which you'll see with the "Ko" removed spells Epke. Removing letters is extremely common, particularly to make names undistinguishable as associated with various ethnic groups, so one might fit in (or hide) and to make it easier to spell or say and quite often as a nickname.

Ed is a popular Jewish name for men. That has always puzzled me. In German "Eid Genossen" means "oath comrades," which is what Huguenots were known to each other during the Middle Ages, meaning that they were bound to each other by an oath. Could Eid have been shortened to Ed? Does it have anything to do with the ancient brotherhood that has held Jews together for thousands of years? Seems kind of silly for me to think like this but how often do you have a chuckle over names and their meanings that people give to their offspring? Quite often.

 I think that there are probably many people who have both Arabic and Jewish ancestry and don't know it. I'm exploring the notion that the surname "Morris" stems from the root "Moor" and are descendants of the Saracens who invaded Spain. The Latin word for Moor is "Maurus." In Greek it is "Mauros," and in French you may find it as "More." There's an interesting book by Thomas Cahill, he discusses the Golden Age of Spain. During that era Arabs and Jews were more "social."

"Rotenu," is the name the Egyptians gave to the tribes living near the Dead Sea, who were the children of Lot "Lotan." Lot was the nephew of Abraham. In the Bible, in the "Book of Numbers," there are many names like this. It is rather tedious but it's worth looking through, you might get clues.

Lamden means "scholar" or "learned one" in Yiddish. Similar sounding last names *may* have Jewish origins. They could have been altered over the years, and today are Lampkin, Lampson, Lampton, etc.

If I had the Scottish surname of McCabe, I would definitely be considering that I may have ancestral links to the Jewish Maccabee family tree. McCabe is Maccabaeus with letters removed which as I mentioned before was a common practice with ancient Jews. McKay could be a variant. Names in the Jewish Maccabee (Asmonaeans) family are: Mattathias, John, Simon, Judas, Eleazar and Jonathan. Judas was also called Makkabi or Maccabaeus. Mariamne was the last. Mariamne is Greek taken from the Hebrew name of Miriam.

Though *Aben* and *Ibn* is Arabic and means "son of," Sephardic Jews often have it before their name. The Hebrew for "son of" is *Ben.*

Once you start gathering the names of your Jewish ancestors, you might want to check out the website called, FTJP (Family Tree of the Jewish People), powered by ancestry.com. It is extensive and will probably still be available five hundred years from now. The aim of their project is "to centralize the collection of Jewish family trees, to provide a powerful resource to connect individuals researching the same Jewish family branches, to re-connect their families, and to increase interest in Jewish genealogy." The web address is: http://www.jewishgen.org/gedcom/.

On old family trees, you'll often see families who named their son, "Calvin." This child was probably originally named after the theologian John Calvin and his religious movement who were called *Calvinists*. The Dutch Reformed Church, Baptists, Puritans, Quakers and Presbyterians, can trace their roots to the writings of controversial John Calvin. He was one of the *reformers* who led people away from the Catholic Church and later, as well, when people left the Church of England. My belief is that many Crypto-Jews from Holland hid or assimilated within the Dutch Reformed Church. During the 1600s there was a Baptist movement called *Sabbatarian* or *Seventh-day Baptists*. Within the later two groups, you may find your Jewish ancestors who may have been hiding within this Protestant movement. These two groups would have practiced their Sabbath on Saturday, as did the Jews.

"The Crockett name was originally Crocquettaine. The family crossed the Pyrenees sometime during the expulsion of Jews and Moors from Spain and was living in Bayonne and Bordeaux in the 16c, among Judaizers. One branch then emigrated to Scotland, with the transfer of the order of Freemasons, and thence to America, ending up in East Tennessee with the Wataugans, then moving to the Cumberland Settlement." Donald Panther-Yates

Try to let go of the surname that does not sound the least bit Jewish. Don't let one name stop you. If you are reading this book you must have other strong hunches. Besides, in America there are some who believe their original surname is "Williams" when it was originally "Vladovski." The Hebrew name Rochel/Rachel became Rose. Gershenberg became anglicized to Gerson or Gersh. Baruch became Bernie and Herschel became Harold. The very ethnic sounding Jewish name of "Yekotiel" became Leopold. It was very common in America for Jews to change their names. It was still common during the depression era. For many, religion was not as important and at the time they felt that a name could either help you get ahead or hold you back. Ethnic sounding names like "Aronovsky" became Arnell.

The Civil War receives a lot of media attention. Listen to surnames that make it to television, print and Internet media. You may hear a familiar surname in a story about the Civil War and find a link you can follow that will help you fill in your family tree or trigger thoughts that help you to uncover facts about unknown ancestry. Approximately seven thousand recorded Jews fought with the North in the Civil War and approximately three thousand recorded Jews fought for the South. I wonder how many Crypto-Jews fought?

Does your grandmother look Jewish but deny it? She may have been raised that way. Does she act fearful when the subject is mentioned? You'd be fearful too if the Inquisition was after all your family, all your friends, your whole community. Ancestors passed this fear onto their children. To survive, they converted to Christianity and kept their mouths buttoned tightly. Your grandmother may have inherited the fear even though the Inquisition was long ago. But this is no longer the Middle Ages, we are free to explore our heritage, which may be a long forgotten Jewish one.

The Hestor (Hester, Ester, Esther) Fascination Factor

The book of Esther is a very short book in the Bible. You will not find it in the oldest texts, it was added later. In the King James Version, it is only seven pages long. Here's my interpretation of it:

King Ahasuerus reigned from India to Ethiopia. The king's servants said, *"Let there be fair young virgins sought for the king ... And let the maiden which pleaseth the king be queen"* instead of the current queen who was disobedient. Mordecai the Jew had a niece, Esther, who was *"fair and beautiful"* and was brought to the king's house. King Ahasuerus was pleased with Esther and *"preferred her and her maids unto the best place of the house of the women."* Esther's Uncle Mordecai had *"charged her that she should not shew"* her people *"nor her kindred."* And everyday Uncle Mordecai, walked to the court of the women's house to check up on her because he loved her like a daughter. *"And the king loved Esther above all the women, and she obtained grace and favour in his sight more than all the virgins; so that he set the royal crown upon her head, and made her queen instead of Vashti."*

But the king had promoted a man named Haman whom Esther's Uncle Mordecai would not bow to. This infuriated Haman and when told that Mordecai was a Jew *"sought to destroy all the Jews that were throughout the whole kingdom..."*

Thanks to Esther's banquets and her uncle's strategies, eventually Uncle Mordecai prevails - the king touches Jewish Queen Esther with his sepulture and she is granted requests of which she requests the Jews not be killed. Haman and his sons were killed instead.

"The Jews had light, and gladness, and joy, and honour... a feast and a good day. And many of the people of the land became Jews; for the fear of the Jews fell upon them." Queen Esther's story is celebrated in the holiday of Purim. It is a huge celebration in many places including Israel and Amsterdam. The book of Esther states that *"these days should be remembered and kept throughout every generation ... these days of Purim should not fail from among the Jews, nor the memorial of them perish from their seed."* Purim begins at sundown on March 9th.

While doing research for my first book, *Secret Genealogy*, I ran across a well-written book by Steven Nadler called "Rembrandt's Jews." In it, Nadler speaks about this story of Esther the Jewess and how during the Middle Ages, Amsterdam's Portuguese Jews saw in Esther, their own Marrano experience of being *"forced to hide their Jewishness."* The medieval Dutch loved to go to and produce plays about Esther. The Jews had their Esther Purim plays, but kept Esther's name out of the title. The Dutch included Hester in the title and "went out of their way to make sure that no one missed the contemporary relevance of the drama," Nadler says.

In the Philippines a holiday is celebrated in May that is reminiscent of the Dutch and their Hester Festival. It's called the "Santacruzan"; it is "celebrated more as a social festival than as a religious ceremony." The festival is a celebration in remembrance of the "recovery of the Holy Cross" by the mother of Constantine Empress Helen of the Byzantine Empire. The chief characters are "*Infanta* Judity, *Reina Sentenciada* (condemned Queen), *Reina Ester* (Queen Esther), *Reina de las Flores* (Queen of Flowers) and *Reina Helena* (Queen Helen) – and their respective *zagalas* (ladies in waiting). The queens are the chosen beauties of the town or from elsewhere, and the loveliest among them is the *Reina Helena*. A boy-king, Constantine, marches by the side of the *Reina Helena*." Judith is a popular Jewish name and of course Esther is present as well. Interesting that the "loveliest" is Queen Helena, my guess is that she would be representative of the Greek influence as the name Helena comes from the word Hellene. But then again, an old Webster's dictionary defines Hellenist as "one who affiliates with Greeks, or imitates Greek manners; esp., a Jew who used the Greek language as his mother tongue."

Chapter Three

Banta, Bandi, Bonte, Bani & the Earliest Dutch Settlement in Indonesia

Bani-Israel means *Children of Israel.* The Beni-Israel are Jews who settled in Bombay, India with records dating back to at least the 12th century. Though they are now Muslim, living in Pakistan and Afghanistan, their history is that they were taken from their desert homeland and their oral history tells of a shipwreck near Bombay necessitating that they settle there. They have a legend that Jesus did not die on the cross but traveled to the Kashmir valley searching for the Ten Tribes and it was there he died. The Bani-Israel continue to marry only amongst themselves, light candles on the Jewish Sabbath and have other customs and characteristics that are very Jewish. Another group of Jews in Southern India are the *Cochin*. Their most popular oral history tells of King Solomon's trading ventures with India's Malabar Coast. King Solomon's sailors and merchants are said to have taken Indian women as wives thus creating the Cochin Jews.

Clues come to us from everywhere. Early one Sunday morning, I was listening to a story on NPR about a woman who had published a book of photographs all taken in Africa. She mentioned that she chose the title of her book based on a Swahili word that meant "togetherness," "all people" and that word was "ubuntu," which sounded similar to Banta, Bonte, Bonta, Bondi, etc. The word "ubuntu" has broad philosophical meaning to a wide range of people living in Africa. The word implies people connectedness, humanness and treating others with dignity and respect. It is an important word to the Bantu people.

"Unlike the Negroes of N. America, who are of Mandingo and allied stocks, those of Brazil are largely Bantu, their ancestors having been brought from Angola."
Grolier Encyclopedia, Vol. 15 & 16, pg. 8

Just because I can't piece it all together doesn't mean I can't share with you the pieces that I have of the Bantu puzzle. All these images conjure up visuals of Africa, India, Indonesia, Dutch Explorers, Portuguese, Muslims and Jews just for starters. I picture Portuguese ships sailing into Indonesia. On board are well educated Sephardic Jews, excellent at navigation with extensive networks both on the seas and with shipping magnates in their offices in Portugal. After the Jews were betrayed by the king of Portugal they fled north to Amsterdam and using their inside information, shared the secret Indonesian spice routes with the medieval *merchant elite* of Holland. Now Dutch ships are sailing into what becomes Banten or Bantam harbor. Where the name for the harbor originated, I have not yet seen. But what pushes me on is that I can't help but wonder if all the versions of Beni, Bantu, Bantam, Banten, Banta, Bonte, Bani, Bandi, and Bonde ... aren't somehow related and their root meaning, "Children of Israel." Perhaps I'm wrong about this but when I follow false clues I learn an incredible amount. Here are my worthy clues and as much supporting information I could obtain.

"Bantu" means "the people" and is used to define numerous African tribes with a variety of dialects. My old encyclopedia states that most of the black people *"living in equatorial and southern Africa (except the Pigmies) belong to the great Bantu family. It is believed that originally the Bantus lived in Eastern Africa and at some later period pushed their way south and west."* Taking a look at my globe I see that the Bantu people could have come from the Holy Land thus making them Bani-Israel, *Children of Israel.* And if there is a connection that could mean that the thousands of people who have similar names (Beni, Bantu, Bantam, Banten, Banta, Bonte, Bani, Bandi, Bonde...) might be part of this huge group. According to the same Grolier Encyclopedia, the languages of black Africans fall into five major groups: Bushman, Bantu, Sudanic, Hamitic and Semitic. The Bantu group has 400 languages.

Being the genealogist that I am, I continue researching the surname "Banta" and find many variations. The name and its variations pop up everywhere and I believe the surname deserves discussion. Even the dictionary I use is the Scribner-*Bantam* English Dictionary from *Bantam* Books in New York. Research leads me to believe that many of these different variations of the surname Banta/Bonte are attempts to keep a link to *Jewish identity.*

I found an interesting legal brief on the Internet stating that the son of Jean Rothschild who changed his surname to "Bonta" had been awarded money from a Swiss bank account that had been lost to the Nazis. I've seen it mentioned that "Bento" stems from "Baruch" which means blessed in Hebrew. World-famous medieval Jewish philosopher, Baruch Spinoza's original Portuguese name was "Bento de Espinosa." Today the surname Banta is seen all around the world. I looked at the phonebook pages for Israeli names and there were plenty of Bantas.

There are over 10,000 Americans with the surname Banta and they are all purported to have begun with the first Banta, in Holland who in 1640, begins to sign his name as "Jacobi Epkes te Bonta." Eventually "Jacobi" was dropped and today the surname lives on as "Banta." His descendant immigrated to New Amsterdam (NY) and was using the name Epke Jacobse. He soon loses the Jacobse and calls himself Banta or Bonte. Why dump Jacobse? Too Jewish? But what was the significance of Banta/Bonte? Some in the family have said it comes from a farm called Bonta or Bonte where he had resided in Friesland. Another said it comes from an island near Friesland. But as I study Dutch history I see that "Bantam" was the first Dutch settlement on the north coast of West Java, the Dutch East Indies.

"Like many politicians who boast of their own candor, Wilders keeps much of his life and work in the shadows. Apart from the boilerplate official biography that says he was raised a Roman Catholic in the town of Venlo, there's little on the record from him about his family background, and he flatly refuses to talk about it now. According to his brother, some of the family's roots extend deep into Indonesia, an outpost of the Dutch

colonialist empire for nearly three and a half centuries. Long-ago intermarriage between European settlers and native 'inlanders' might possibly account for the slightly almond shape of Wilder's dull-blue eyes."
Newsweek, Jan 23, 2012, "Can't Someone Tell Geert Wilders To Stop His Anti-Muslim Diatribes Before Somebody Gets Hurt?" by Christopher Dickey

During the 1600s, when Dutch merchants, got a hold of the secrets of Portugal's spice routes, many of these Dutch merchants were Sephardic Jews who kept their ethnicity hidden, or at least tried to, and were referred to as *Portuguese Merchants*, although to many in Amsterdam, it was quite obvious they were Jews who'd fled the Inquisition. The knowledge Portuguese Merchants acquired then brought north, helped bring about the wealth of Holland's *Golden Era*. The knowledge of Portugal's secret spice routes led to the Dutch going to Banten (Bantam) Province, West Java, and it became an important trading port. West Java and the South Pacific islands were a tropical paradise. One can only imagine how enamored the Dutch must have been.

Today there are remains of the ancient "Islamic Banten Kingdom." The website that shared this information (http://indonesiacultures.com/banten.html) states that Banten was *"once a powerful maritime capital"* and that during the reign of Sultan Agung 1651-1683, *"Banten experienced its golden era. Unfortunately when Sultan Agung of Banten fell, the Dutch began to take over."*

You might be thinking, Banten is Islamic, end of story ... but remember the Beni-Israel of India converted to Islam yet still preserve their ancient oral history and many customs of their original Jewish faith. In Banten, eventually the Muslim rulers did some double-dealing with both the Dutch and the English and a gruesome fight broke out. The Dutch prevailed and renamed the area "Batavia." The Dutch exploited the natives. Their plan was to make plantations and enslave or kill off the natives. Wealthy Dutch built canals and houses that resembled those they left behind in Holland. Indonesian and Chinese immigrants (slaves?) crowded the area, perhaps sometimes intermarrying with the Dutch, which would bring Indonesian and Chinese ancestry into one's family tree. Note that Batavia was occupied by Japan during WWII and renamed Jakarta. Today the area is known as Indonesia but the Dutch knew it as West Java.

South of the African Cameroons there were Bantus during the 1950s who were still primitive. And last but certainly not least, Banta is also the name of a butterfly and the name of a popular soda pop in India.

Chapter Four

Our Hellenistic Jewish Ancestors

I love the process by which our ancestors rise from their graves like the sand man in the movie Spiderman. It always amazes me how alive they are, like seeds lying in ancient tombs waiting for us to water them. The seeds of our ancestors, when we are on the right track, are so viable, it's amazing how quickly they sprout.

Many ancient Jews loved the Greek culture and emulated it as best they could. An old Webster's dictionary defines Hellenist as "one who affiliates with Greeks, or imitates Greek manners; esp., a Jew who used the Greek language as his mother tongue." And the Greek rulers were also influenced by Jewish culture. Even the word Diaspora is the Greek word for "a scattering." The Jews loved Alexandria, the Egyptian city along the Mediterranean, famous for it's history dating back more than three hundred years before the Christian era. During that ancient era, Alexandria was the center of culture and knowledge. Founded by Alexander the Great, Alexandria is known for such notable historical figures as Mark Anthony and Cleopatra.

Philo (20 BCE - 40 CE) of Alexandria was an influential Hellenized Jew who laid the foundations for Christianity. Philo was a founder of religious philosophy; he was very well educated in Greek philosophy and culture, with the highest regard for the teachings of the Jewish prophet Moses. The word philosophy is made of two Greek words, it means *love of wisdom*.

Helling, Hellingh, Hellmich and Helm are just a few of the surnames that could signify Greek or *Jewish identity*. In German, "mich" means "I am." So Hellmich means, "I am Hell" which I believe means, I am Hellenistic, I am Greek. There were Hellings who were Huguenots from France and oftentimes Jews posed as Huguenots or joined them.

A little research on some ancient Jews, who loved all things Greek, is revealed in the following quotes from Berel Wein adapted by Yaakov Astor:

"At its height, Alexandria was the wealthiest, most powerful, most influential and most sophisticated Jewish community. The Talmud describes a synagogue of immense proportions that the community built. Jewish artisans of Alexandria each had their own section in the synagogue: the goldsmiths sat in one section, the silversmiths in another, and the carpenters in a third." ... "Josephus writes that the synagogue was like an amphitheater. It had 8-10,000 seats. It was so large that people in one part could not hear the service taking place in the same room in another part, so in order to answer "Amen" they raised flags and waved." (http://www.jewishhistory.org/the-hell-in-hellenism/)

The history of the Jews who loved Greek culture is elaborated upon in the above mentioned website of Jewish history. One point they made was that in 200 B.C.E., a large population of Jews abandoned their Jewish culture, especially the upper class, calling themselves "Misyavnim" which meant "Hellenists." "The Greeks found many willing collaborators among the Jews in their attempt to eradicate Judaism and install the more 'enlightened' pagan culture of theirs in Israel. These Hellenist Jews hated their brethren and openly sided with the enemies of Israel who attempted to destroy the Jewish nation and faith."

It's very difficult to explain history that stems back thousands of years but the Jewish roots of *some* of our Christian ancestors may have been that of the Hellenists. There are probably Rabbis in some Christian family trees as well. Rabbis who became priests instead of being burned at the stake. But if our Jewish ancestors were Hellenists, who loved Greek culture, you will sometimes find it in their names. I have an ancestral surname of Helling, an uncle born a hundred years ago has the Greek name of Solon and my name, Suellen, as southern as it sounds, has its root in the Greek Hellen. It could be I had ancestors who were *Alexandrian Jews*.

25

History may show that once upon a time there were Jews who rose against other Jews. But we cannot know if our ancestors belonged to that sect or were simply Jews who embraced Greek culture. I cannot speak for people who are dead thousands of years back. We are speaking of the era before Christianity.

If you have the surname "Alexander," it could be a Jewish surname, linked to the history of Alexandria. I found this at http://en.wikipedia.org/wiki/Jewish_name:

"There was some objection to foreign names among the Jews of this period, yet legend declares that the high priest Simon promised Alexander the Great that all the children of priestly families born in the year following his visit to Jerusalem would be named Alexander, after him."

There are varying degrees of devotion including a complete devotion to Judaism by Jews who did not turn away from their religion and instead chose death, as was the case for thousands of Jews during Inquisitional times. But it appears that many Jews quite simply were fatigued of persecution and taxes and outwardly chose to blend into the majority population, especially in the New World. But please, ***never underestimate the fact that Jews were killed just for being Jews. I believe the fact that their lives were in danger was the number one reason our Jewish ancestors hid their ethnicity.***

It can be dangerous to be a Jew. Yet often, those who would do them harm are of Jewish ethnicity themselves. I find that paradox astounding. When racial hate brought about forced abandonment of Judaism, or necessitated a cryptic lifestyle, it is no wonder descendants are unaware of Jewish ethnicity. But could our Jewish ancestors imagine a time when their descendants would discriminate against them?

Chapter Five

Blood Types

When I wrote the first *Secret Genealogy*, I mentioned that I thought it might help fight anti-Semitism if people reconnected to their Semitic past. There is no *us* and *them*. The more one explores history the more one understands the interconnectedness between the people of the world. Humans started out in the area of Africa and the Middle East. They migrated in every direction then many migrated back. For example, Egyptians and other Middle Easterners may have "Germanic" DNA because "Ancient Germans" traveled south to the Taurus Mountain ranges and merged with the pre-Hittites, later becoming Hittites and having a substantial empire that sometimes included Egypt and Syria. This is what I mean by there is no *us* and *them.* Some believe there are genetically exclusive Jews among the Priestly Cohen class, purported to be of direct patrilineal descent from the Biblical Aaron but other than this *perhaps* instance, no one is pure anything. Anti-Semitic groups would like to think so but are ignorant if they do not understand that they have the same blood diversity flowing through their veins as the rest of us. Through *Google Alerts*, I receive great articles about various historical groups, including the Cochin, Ethiopian, Spanish and Italian Jews as well as other Crypto-Jewish groups rediscovering their ancient roots. Although orthodox Jews are expected to marry other Jews, it is my understanding they may marry one who has fully converted to Judaism. The ancient Khazars have a fascinating Jewish ancestral history and are examples of converts to Judaism.

What is life if you can't have fun? This chapter is just that. Made up of what I garnered from the Internet and am sharing it because ... well just because it's fun and maybe there might be some tidbit that triggers one's mind or imagination and leads to an entirely different discovery. I'm going to focus on O negative blood type because after conducting a little Internet research to see what was being said, I noticed the discussions included Jewish ethnicity, though most Jews are not O negative. Some of these sources have no way of verification because they are so "out there." But I have an incredible imagination and an open mind and enjoyed reading it.

Blood banks love donors with O negative blood because it is compatible with any blood type. It is sought after for babies needing exchange and for accident victims. Rh O- negative blood type is extremely rare in China and Japan. If that is your blood type you may consider this before deciding to venture there, as you would have a difficult time if you needed a transfusion.

A woman with O-negative blood and the Rh-factor, after the birth of her first child, must have a shot of rhogam. If this shot were not taken within so many hours after her first birth, the mother's second child would need a blood transfusion if the baby's father and mother have "incompatible blood types." Without that rhogam shot, the mother could have what's referred to as a "blue baby" and the child could die without a blood transfusion. While combing through genealogical records, I have seen instances of a mother being pregnant 16 times and losing 6 or 7 of the infants which got me to thinking, *were these deaths due to incompatible blood types before the advent of drugs to prevent it?* The unborn child's blood cells can get into the mother's blood during birth, if they are incompatible, the mother will develop antibodies and reject the unborn child's blood.

According to the website, www.med.unc.edu/obgyn/rh.htm, "scientists are not sure of the origins of this Rh-Negative factor, some saying it is a mutation that came about over 25,000 years ago in Europe. The highest rates of Rh-negative blood occur in the Basque populations of France and Spain, perhaps as high as close to one-third the population and close to two-thirds of Basque population carrying one of the (r) negative genes."

Another group having high percentages of this Rh-Negative factor are the Oriental Jews of Israel, which is unique because among the

Chinese and Japanese, it is almost non-existent, maybe one out of a hundred people.

The Black Cochin Jewish population has a high percentage of Rh-negative blood but the Rh-negative blood type is uncommon in the Black population in general. Which is exactly the same interesting phenomenon as with the Asian population as mentioned above.

The Samaritans also have a higher occurrence of Rh-negative blood. Yes, I asked the same question, *but who are the Samaritans?* The Samaritans appear to be the descendants of Jews and Gentiles from the Holy Land. They used the books of Moses (the Torah) but instead of focusing their worship toward Jerusalem it was toward a Samarian mountain. Their history is related to the ancient Kingdom of Judea.

Other Researchers speak about the incidence of high percentages of Rh-factor among the Moroccan Berbers. There are varying opinions about the ethnicity of the Berbers. Some are fair skinned while others are black. Today Berbers are Islamic but some say they were originally Jewish or Christian. One account I read said the Berbers were descendants of concubines and slaves who had been transported to North Africa. A Morocco travel bureau said the Berbers "have been called by many names: Libyans by the ancient Greeks, Numbians, and Africans by the Romans and Moors by medieval Europe. In fact, it was the Arabs who came up with the Berber name. Islam came to the Berbers in the ninth and tenth centuries. Prior to then, most Berbers across Africa were Christian or Jewish. Two great Islamic Berber dynasties, Almoravids and Almohads, ruled large parts of Spain and northwest Africa."

With the Basques holding such a high percentage of their population having Rh-negative blood compared to others in Europe, when studied extensively it was found that along the Spanish border there is a very noticeable genetic contrast between the Basque and the Spanish. Yet along the French border these genetic differences are not as distinct, showing that the Basque and descendants of the Basque have more heavily populated those areas into France than those of Spain.

If the Rh-negative factor is a mutation, it is believed by some to have happened in the Basque European homeland maybe 40,000 years ago. The "race" of the Basques is debated heavily, some even questioning if they are Caucasian, others going to great lengths to prove they are ... drum roll here ... "reptilian." Still, others go much further and question if Rh-negative blood types are the descendants of "ancient astronauts," quoting various passages from the Old Testament to prove their hypothesis.

Because the Basque have a language that does not tie in with any other European tongue, these Basque conspiracy theorists ask if it wasn't *"the original language of the book of Genesis," "of the world"* and *"possibly of the creator."* I like that much better than reptilian reference, not that I have anything against cold-blooded lizards and snakes. Although my college biology professor told of the evolution of humans originating from a great primordial soup where we were one-celled organisms, then eventually fish-like amphibians that later developed into our lovely human selves.

Then there are those who believe that Rh-negative is the *"total pure unbroken bloodline of the tribe of Judah"* and that Jesus was a Rho-Neg, as were *"all the Ancient Hebrews."*
I don't know how someone would know Noah and his descendants blood type but they state that they do and that, *"Noah and his descendants were all Rh-O- negatives."*

It is disconcerting to believe that people might be prejudice against those with the Rh-factor. The Nazis were into blood types, trying to use anything they could for proof of superior and inferior races. The Nazis tattooed blood types upon the bodies of some of their top brass. I suppose the thinking was to enable medics to quickly and correctly treat their soldiers on the battlefield but it would not surprise me if it were to make sure their top military personnel were not "contaminated" with any of the blood types of those they believed inferior.

I ran across conversations about Rh-negative blood types among British Royalty. The statements contradicted each other and there was a large amount of information so if you are interested in the blood types of British Royalty you'll have to attempt that yourself. But I must warn you, you'll have to sort through the *Reptilian Conspiracy*.

"The more we study the precise details of human variation, the more we understand how complex are the patterns. They cannot be easily summarized or understood. Yet, this hard-earned scientific knowledge is generally ignored in most countries because of more demanding social and political concerns. As a result, discrimination based on presumed "racial" groups still continues. It is important to keep in mind that this "racial" classification often has more to do with cultural and historical distinctions than it does with biology. In a very real sense, "race" is a distinction that is created by culture not biology."
Dennis O'Neil   http://anthro.palomar.edu/vary/vary_3.htm

The history of the Christians, Egyptians, Jews, Muslims, Phoenicians, Hittites and others belong to us all. It makes one less xenophobic to know other cultures and to have a direct link to them through our own ancient ancestry. Take for example Banten. If your Dutch, Portuguese or English ancestor took a native of Banten (today's Indonesia) as a spouse and that native was of the former Islamic Banten Kingdom, it means you have an ancient Indonesian Islamic ancestor. What genealogist wouldn't love that information? We can spend years uncovering ancient "bloodlines" but if it becomes a source of seeking for superiority, I believe one is on the wrong track. This author does not see any ethnic group or groups as superior of others.

Chapter Six

Jews in European Countries Outside the Holy Land

What ethnicity are we? Good question. What is it, the last nation with which you were a citizen of? And then what nation is that nation? The last country that conquered it? America's boundaries did a lot of changing during the Colonial era and so have countries around the world. It may seem interesting to ask that question of one who has a foreign accent but they may have been a citizen of *our* country long before *we* were born, so to them it could make us appear racist.

One new aspect that I find surprising is how non-exclusive many of our ancient Jewish ancestors were. Except for periods when Jews were rounded up into ghettos and death camps, there is no reason to exclude them from a variety of European histories. Jews fought in Roman Legions and though perhaps cryptically, were settlers in merry Old England. They were the athletes in the Greek games. They were spiritual teachers of many eras. They were amongst those who danced and partook of the decadent feasts and lifestyles of the ancient kingdoms of Egypt and Babylon. They aligned with the Hittites and the Phoenicians on projects much the same way we form alliances with other nations today. Jews were kings, princes, queens and princesses. When descendants of royalty fell into poverty, they may have resorted to rag peddling, but they persevered and took advantage of opportunities (moving to other countries) and lived to see their children again rise in stature. Everyone is not of Jewish ancestry, although it sometimes appears so when you become clued in. Through the centuries of art, poetry, literature math and science, we see ourselves. Through an openness and honesty toward all ethnicities and their ancient pasts, we learn from one another, we learn about ourselves and our origins of long ago. The world encompasses a large area but as we've heard many times ... it truly is ... *a small world.*

How did I get started? When I was visiting England for the first time, my husband and I visited two English villages within a day's ride of one another. The villages carried the names of *Hose* and *Wroughton*. Both of our surnames, although my husband's surname, Hose is Jewish. In the registry of the small, ancient church dated 1109, at the Village of Hose; the first minister's name was Eliya, bringing thoughts of the well-loved prophet of the Old Testament, Elija. The successive ministers had surnames but not Eliya. The registry had only his first name. The village had no knowledge why it was named Hose. On the way to the village there was a small hand-painted sign in the middle of the woods. One sign had a directional arrow with the village name "Hose," the other arrow pointing in the opposite direction toward "Nottingham." My mind soared with images of Robin Hood and Sherwood Forest of long ago. My husband joked, *"It wasn't Robin Hood, it was Robin Hose."* There was a street sign nearby that referenced the Holy Land. Then in Nottingham we visited an old medieval pub called, "Ye Olde Trip to Jerusalem." It was in that pub that men were liquored up then recruited into marching to Jerusalem to fight in the Crusades. The area had a strong ancient connection to the Holy Land. My mind began a fictional story about a love affair between a Christian from the Village of Wroughten and a Jew from the Village of Hose. A historical romance in my head had begun and I started writing *The Celtic Prince*. Once I started researching, I was shocked to discover that my fantasy began to become reality. I was hooked. I started seeing that my father's surname of Wroten had Jewish roots. Of course, Rotenberg is very Jewish. Who would have thought? Not me, ever. Nor had my Jewish father-in-law whose son I had been married to for almost twenty-five years. Further researching into old census records revealed the name in the 1700s had been spelled Roten. Then I remembered my father had said he thought that it had originally had a berg or stein on the end of it. Even now as I write this, I shake my head. How could we miss something this important?

And it works both ways. Research into my father-in-law's genealogy reveals he had non-Jews in his tree. Our ancestry is not exclusive to one ethnicity or the other, at least not entirely. I began my novel by researching heavily. *The Celtic Prince*, became a story about the hardships of the ancient world and the difficult subject of ethnicity. And though entirely fiction, I got a lot of ideas from my patriarchal ancestry. It gave me somewhere to start. After I finished I thought I would write another novel with ideas from my matriarchal family line. Well surprise, surprise. I would have never thought my mother, a simple girl from Kansas descended from prominent French Huguenots and Dutch Jews who married Eastern European women and immigrated to Colonial America. Jews? These Christian, Anglo-Saxon, Protestants? No! Yes. Shock, shock, shock. My mother's ancestors became a treasure trove of material. In no small part did these "Dutch" "French" "Frisian" Crypto-Jews help build the earliest Dutch settlement in America's Colony, New Amsterdam. This created the backdrop for another historical novel, *"The Lies of the Lion,"* where I attempt, through fiction, to explain how through centuries of trial, terror and traditions lost, Jews became Christians. And my husband began to tease me, "You're more Jewish than I am."

When I saw the names of the close associates of my mother's ancestors, I began to see a conspiracy. And when I paired it with the fact that both my mother and father's "people" were deeply embedded into Freemasonry, I began to believe that there must be a connection between the Masons and Crypto-Jews. *Was that what was so secret?* A haven from the outside world? A group sworn to secrecy where they could create their own style of worship and a bond so strong none would tell? A third novel was born, *The Guild - Hester's Goodwill*, attempting to explain my suspicions.

So here I am with *Secret Genealogy II*. There was no way I was going to waste all the research I did for the novels. Currently I am delving deeply into Colonial American History and will continue writing novels, and though it is tedious, more *Secret Genealogy* books.

I can't believe how much I'm right about clues, much more than I would have thought. I am shocked at what I find and my hunches began in late 2003. I feel like a child whose grown-ups around her have led another life, keeping secrets with a wink and a nod or in desperation for fear of the nightmare that followed them from Spanish and Portuguese stadiums into the New World.

As I mentioned earlier, it appears the British Royal Family has ancient Jewish ancestry. They are mostly silent about it, which leaves me breathless to think that a family with the wealth, power and prestige of the Royal House of Windsor, would in this day and age be cautious of the repercussions such a discussion would bring about. The world is full of folks with Jewish ancestry; even anti-Semites should take a better look at their family tree. Aren't most of us a little bit of everything? Isn't it time we were pleased about that?

During the early 1600s, Haarlem Holland offered the Jews a burial ground and a promise to not oppressive them. The offer was probably due to the fact that wealth and prosperity soon followed when Jews settled into communities and left when they were driven out. So is it no surprise that ancestors whom we suspect may have been Jewish, would name their New World community "Haarlem"? And though they are listed as "Christian," should it be a surprise that many of the communities where our suspected Jewish ancestors settled, attracted thousands of Jews and today are strong Jewish communities?

As traveling agriculturalists, vendors, dignitaries, prophets and peasants, the Jews have endured for thousands of years. For a variety of reasons, we have tall blonde Jews, redheaded Jews, black-haired Jews, etc. The term Diaspora refers to the fact that after their exile from Jerusalem the Jews scattered throughout the world. They went to Greece, Spain, Portugal, France, Japan, Egypt, India, Afghanistan, Italy, Malta, Pakistan, Germany, the Netherlands, Iran, Iraq, Africa, China, Russia, the British Isles, the West Indies, Ceylon, Mauritius, Australia, Borneo, Formosa, North and South America, the list goes on. Communities of Jews still exist in many of these countries. You can find websites specializing in Jewish ancestry in various countries, many having copies of ancient records.

"In early England they were treated with a certain rough justice, cruelly interrupted by "popular" riot and massacre, such as occurred at the coronation of Richard I. After that dire experience the English Jewry was reorganized, but their expulsion in 1290 followed when the inroad of Lombard bankers rendered the Jews no longer financially necessary." Grolier Encyclopedia

London's Lombard Street is a lot like America's Wall Street. Over 800 years ago, the Lombards who settled here were moneylenders, giving this London area special historical significance. Who were the Lombards? Their original name, *Langobardi* may mean "*men of the long axes*." The Lombards were members of ancient European Teutonic tribes. The Teutonics were defined as tall and blonde and included many other northern European groups. In 568 the Lombards conquered Northern Italy, and contributed to the history of Moravia as it was there they became Arians adapting the doctrine that Christ was not the eternal Son of God nor of that essence. Northern Italy still bears their name, Lombardy.

I did not begin researching Jewish ancestry for my own family. Why would I? We weren't Jews. I was doing it as a hobby for my husband's family but in the act of being thorough, I would always check to see if my maiden name happened to be upon one of the Jewish lists of names. One day I ran across the name Rotin and its connection to the ancient Spanish Kingdom of Murcia. Just the "stuff" fairy tales are made of. I became instantly immersed into the world of European Jewry and ancient Hebrew and Biblical stories with my ancestors as part of the plot. Rotin is an ancient Jewish name contained in medieval documents from the Kingdom of Murcia and Murcia is an ancient province in Southeastern Spain. This information was found through the website www.sephardim.com. I highly suggest that this is the place to begin.

Am I the only one who thinks twice when hearing Georgia in the news? The United States has the state of Georgia and then we have

Georgia, the state in the Caucasus region of Eurasia whose oral history proclaims they descend from Noah's son Japheth although today many are Muslim. The small Eurasian state of Georgia has had short histories of independence and became a Russian province after seeking Russia's help during the 1600s when there were wars raging between the Persians and Turks. Today, the former Russian republic of Georgia continues to make world news.

Holland today is as much a hotbed for ethnic diversity as it was during the Middle Ages. If you want interesting history, one is lucky to have ancestry that came through Holland. Because of Holland's northern location, many descendants of Jews are unaware of their Semitic Dutch origins. There is no reason one must give up Dutch heritage in order to embrace Jewish heritage. Medieval Jewish men of the north probably looked like all others, bundled in furs, living the same lifestyle, much the same culture, especially if they were Cryptic-Jews.

My research leads me to believe that though they kept their identity cryptic, Jews found comfort and security in northern areas of the Netherlands centuries before the Inquisitions. During and after the Inquisitions, Jews made their homes in Amsterdam, hiding behind the facade of being *Portuguese Merchants*, and with the exception of World War II, managed to survive and prosper. Today there are large populations of Jews living in Holland and plenty of descendants of Crypto-Jews who either don't know of their heritage or are content with the assimilation their ancestors chose.

There was a cultural separation between the Sephardic Jews and the Ashkenazic Jews of medieval Holland. The Sephardic Jews, who fled to Holland from Spain and Portugal and referred to as *Portuguese Merchants*, were often affluent with extensive networks built during their years in Spain and Portugal, while the Ashkenazic were often poor, less fortunate peddler types. I've seen it written that the Sephardim did not want the Ashkenaz buried in their cemeteries. But these petty differences seemed to dissipate and the future saw the tables turned when Ashkenaz Jews became more prosperous than the Sephardim whose networks and industries collapsed due to the changing politics of international commercial ventures. It may be hard to distinguish Sephardim from Ashkenaz on an ancient family tree but one may find Sephardic *Portuguese Merchants* married women with Eastern European sounding names. Dutch Sephardic Jews tend to have more Latin names while Ashkenzic Jews have more Germanic, Eastern European names. During Amsterdam's *Golden Era*, large populations of Ashkenazim immigrated into Holland to partake of the many flourishing industries, which were often built upon the networks of the *Portuguese Merchants.*

"The Jews suffered from persecution during the Middle Ages. The first Jews came to London in 1096 as refugees from Rouen after a massacre occurred there. Jews in London lived in a ghetto in old Jewry. They were some of the first people since Roman times to live in stone houses. They had to as wooden houses were not safe enough! In 1189 a wave of persecution resulted in the deaths of about 30 Jews. In 1264 rioters killed about 500 Jews in London. Then in 1290 all Jews were expelled from England." Tim Lambert
http://www.localhistories.org/london.html

England has a rich Jewish history. Jews have been on British soil for thousands of years. They were there before the Romans and have had a continued presence since, sometimes assimilating into the main population and religion. But there were those who were discrete, practicing Judaism only in secret. During eras when Jews were not allowed to dwell in England, wealthy Jews managed to take up residence. We know this because they show up in historical records. The term "French Jews" was used during the 1700s in London, in neighborhoods that were attractive to both Jews and Huguenots. During the 1800s thousands of Jews immigrated to England where they have built strong communities.

During the early 1400s, Italians turned silk making into the main trade for Lyons, France where Jews had been since ancient

Romans brought them as prisoners. This silk industry spread throughout the southeast of France then spread to London during the 1600s where Huguenot refugee silk weavers fled and established workshops in the neighborhoods of Bethnal Green, Shoreditch and Spitalfields. These "Huguenot" silk weavers may very well have been Jews posing as Huguenots. In Old London many traditional occupations required affiliations with a guild of which many Jews were excluded.

When we speak of the *Low Germans* we speak of the areas near the North Sea, which takes me to an important geographical area of my earlier research. As I mentioned in *Secret Genealogy*, my belief is that during the middle ages there were Jews residing in the Leeuwarden, Friesland area. But let me also note that I was told by a *Low Dutch* descendant that as early American colonists they used the term *Low Dutch* to distinguish themselves from the Germans – they wanted it to be clear they were NOT Germans.

"We know one Scotsman whose profile we have seen on Roman coins, and of course the Roman legionaries were recruited from all corners of the Empire – from the plains of Hungary and North Germany, from the Tigris and from North Africa. One Roman emperor was a Negro. So that a considerable amount of new blood entered the British racial stock during the Roman occupation, as at all other times in their long history." EVERYDAY LIFE IN ROMAN AND ANGLO-SAXON TIMES, pg 24, by Marjorie and C.H.B. Quennell, Dorset Press, 1987.

When we speak of Celts we often get a variety of images. One image is of the Celtic Festivals springing up celebrating the cultures of Scotland and Ireland. But the history of the Celts (Kelt, Celta, Celtae, Keltoi) began in Europe. The Celts are the ones famous for heading into battle naked, adorned only with golden torques about their necks, men with flaming red hair blowing wild and free. Word is they scared the daylights out of the Romans and were able to sack the place, leaving to history the story of the hordes of Barbarians who ruined advanced Roman civilization, driving the world into the dark ages. Interestingly enough, there are instances where the ancients described the Celts as "tall and blonde." Because the group absorbed other groups, the Celts are categorized together as those who speak Celt, which includes the Gauls (France was Gaul originally), the Britons and modern day Irish, Scots, Welsh and Bretons.

You never know where you'll find that next clue. Here is a good example of using middle names to *attempt* to trace our origins. We will use Effie Herrington's middle name of "Lavonia." During the 1400s, Livonia was a state in Eastern Europe. Livonian means "sword-bearing." History tells us that Livonian Knights united with the Teutonic Knights in 1237 but broke the association in 1521. Scandinavian countries, Poland and Russia wanted to reign over this region (Lithuania) but eventually the area was encompassed by Poland. What does this tell me? Effie Herrington's ancestors were proud of the Livonian Knights in the family? Or, more practically but not necessarily accurate, Effie had Eastern European origins. But ... when you have no information on an ancestor, clues like this give you *something* to go on. Then one day you go to the very old cemetery of their descendant and you see that many of the headstones have Eastern European names. But the real spine tingling effect is when you are leaving the cemetery and your husband stops you in the foyer and points to the ground and in the beautiful blue tiles you see the unmistakable *Star of David*.

Today, it is very difficult to look back and "guess" whether an Eastern European ancestor was a German or a Jew, all we can do is look at the clues and speculate. But when you do not know and you see the Star of David in the tiles, it helps.

It is unknown where the ancient Livonians originally came from. They lived along the coast. The history of Livonia is one where the Germans overtook the peasants who had been living there peacefully. During the middle 1500s the Baltic Livonians (Latvians) were farmers and fishermen but to belong to one of the city guilds, it was required that members speak German. In one Livonian area, Courland, Jewish artisans, traders and merchants came to the area in large numbers, depriving the natives of job opportunities. The natives detested the Germans so perceived the Jews as being the natural allies of the German ruling class.

Knowing the history is great but we do not know which "group" our Livonian ancestor belonged but like I said, her descendants were buried in a cemetery where there was a large *Star of David* in the entrance tiles. Lavonia is Latin (Livonia, Livonicus, Lyvones, Livoni, Lyvonia) but a search of a Latin dictionary turned up nothing except "Lavonia, Georgia," a city in the United States. We can look at Lavonia Georgia and see if Effie Lavonia Herrington shows up on an old census. As I mentioned earlier, in the Caucasus region there is another "Georgia," an eastern European territory. One has to wonder if there is any connection between the two Georgias. The history of the Jews in Poland, Russia, Belarus and Germany is legendary. We have these clues: Coast dwellers, Belarus, Slavs, Jewish artisans, Germans and that Lavonia is a Latin name. Sometimes these clues are all we have and we save them for the next generation to decipher.

Over two hundred years ago the Czars of Russia expelled Jews from Moscow and St Petersburg. From 1791 to 1915 they were ordered to remain within certain boundaries known as "The Pale of Settlement." This Pale included Belorussia, Lithuania, Crimea and part of Poland. When early Colonial Jews in New Amsterdam (NY) were told they could not own land or retail businesses nor stand guard against intruders and if they had come from Poland or "The Pale" where they had also not been allowed to own land, it is not surprising Jewish Immigrants kept quiet about their ethnicity. Coming to the New World was very much about acquiring land.

Jewish Civilians During the Destruction of the Warsaw Ghetto, Poland 1943
National Archives Collection of World War II War Crimes Records, 1933 - 1950

After Spain and Portugal's Inquisitions, when Jews were exiled by the thousands, Jews went north, south, east and west. The Jews who went to Italy eventually were forced into Christian baptisms. If they weren't forced into baptisms, they were subjected to priests delivering sermons in their synagogues. The situation was not tolerable and thousands fled. But thousands were baptized and became Christians. I cannot state this enough, *just because your ancestors were Christians does not mean they were not originally Jewish.* The stories told about what happened in Italy to the Jews are atrocious. Those who fled Italy and went to Fez, Morocco were refused by the Moors and died of hunger in the desert. Others were trapped upon disease-ridden ships, after being refused in Fez, so thousands returned to Italy, defeated and forced to accept baptism. There were lucky ones who made it to new lands, including the Ottoman Empire where the Sultan is reputed to have been grateful for receiving them as they "enriched" his lands.

In an article in the Jerusalem Post by Michael Freund, he states "the Jewish presence in Sicily dates back some two thousand years." A *mikva*, (Jewish ritual bath) dating back to the Byzantine period has been found in Syracuse, a Sicilian city along the Mediterranean Sea. "Some historians say the first Jews were brought there as slaves by the victorious Roman legions during the Second Temple period. The community steadily grew in the ensuing centuries despite various periods of persecution, and produced an array of great scholars and rabbis," the author says. "Towards the end of the 14th century, Sicily's Jews were confined to ghettos and faced increasingly harsh decrees as well as massacres and forced conversions to Catholicism." Freund is the Chairman of Shavei Israel (www.shavei.org), a Jerusalem-based organization that assists lost tribes and hidden Jewish communities to return to the Jewish people. "Despite the danger they faced," Freund says, "the crypto-Jews of Sicily and southern Italy persisted in keeping alive the memory of their ancestors and their faith. Many are now coming forward to reclaim it as their own."

Ancient Roman Road

Jews have been in France for thousands of years and the Inquisitions of Spain and Portugal drove many more Jewish immigrants into the area. But thousands of Inquisitional Jews were unable to survive in France without abandoning Judaism. Many Jews went through France *before* going to Amsterdam to disguise the fact that they were fleeing the Inquisitions. Italy and Germany were also used as temporary residences to avoid drawing attention to their plight. Yes, going straight to Holland from Spain or Portugal would have been obvious. How many people are descendants of Jews who *stopped over* in one of these European countries and they show up on ship's records as coming from France, Italy or Germany? So we call our ancestors, French,

Italian, German, etc. but it is often incorrect. Why not know the truth?

The movie, "Sarah's Key," based on the book by Tatiana de Rosnay, brings to mind a more recent era of Jewish persecution in France. But today France is said to have the largest Jewish community in Europe and more kosher restaurants than New York City. There are many prominent Jews in the fields of medicine, entertainment, business and the arts. World-renown rabbis reside in France where Jews are free to practice Judaism.

"A Jewish presence existed in France during the Roman period, but the community mainly consisted of isolated individuals, rather than an established community. After the Roman conquest of Jerusalem, boats filled with Jewish captives landed in Bordeaux, Arles and Lyons. Archeological finds of Jewish objects with menorahs imprinted on them date back to the first through fifth century."
Rebecca Weiner - The Virtual Jewish History Tour, France

So please understand that if you have French ancestry and are having a hard time finding ancestral trails it may be because they were Jewish. During the middle 1600s there were large populations of Jewish immigrants from Poland who went to France. Most of these immigrants were likely Ashkenazic. You may recognize them on family trees because of their European sounding names. During the 1700s, in Paris, the wealthier Sephardic Jews settled on the Left Bank of the Seine River while the Ashkenazim settled on the Right Bank of the river. Bordeaux, in southwestern France was historically a Sephardic community where Jews fled north from Spain and Portugal, coming over the treacherous Pyrenees Mountains. Bordeaux was near the coast, making it easy to flee if necessary.

It is a fair question to ask if one's French Huguenot ancestors were Jewish. The growth of the Protestant movement added to the religious turmoil of the era. Some believe it helped bring on the

44

Inquisitions. Protestants, Jews and Moors were persecuted. But many Jews hid behind the Huguenot Maltese cross and certainly Jewish DNA is to be found amongst the Huguenots. I read that Charlie Chaplin was of Huguenot ancestry yet he was buried in a Jewish cemetery. Interesting.

When we pass, we will leave genealogical work for our descendants to sort through. But it will be a new era with access to highly advanced technology. Today there is still a lot of work to do. There are old papers lying around. Our family trees are like quilts with pieces from all over the globe. Like jigsaw puzzles with the pieces spread all over the table little by little, we piece them together. It is who we are. Who we were. It is who we are to become. And all these puzzle pieces are connected. Genealogists understand this. We are one family. Very distant cousins perhaps but definitely one family.

Ancient homes near Amsterdam's Old Portuguese Synagogue

Chapter Seven

America's Southern Jewish Clues

The history of Jews in America's early colonies intrigues me. As a descendant of Colonial settlers on both my mother and father's side, I have lots of ancestry who lived in the south. Their history will take me a lifetime to explore and with my interest in both Caucasian and African American southern history my research takes me along many untraveled roads, roads that intersect and roads that go for eternity.

For those of you who have not read my first book, *Secret Genealogy*, I would like to make it clear that if you have ancestors who go back to the early colonies of New Amsterdam or New Spain, your Jewish ancestors had good reason to hide. In 1650 Jews in New Amsterdam were still not allowed to trade freely, could not own land, could not operate a retail or wholesale establishment nor could the men help defend the colony. The New World was not the land of opportunity for Jews while Governor Stuyvesant was in control. But by 1664, Jews were allowed to colonize openly when New Amsterdam became an English colony. In New France it was not the case.

Modeled after laws created in 1685, for French Caribbean colonies, the French released the *Black Code of Louisiana* in 1724. Designed to regulate relations between New World Colonists and their Slaves, the first law in the *Black Code* was the "expulsion of Jews" from the Louisiana Colony. In other words, *Jews are not welcome in Louisiana*. Is it no wonder our southern ancestors kept secret about their origins or that today one's relatives might be subconsciously uncomfortable mentioning Jewish ancestry?

During Inquisitional periods, Jews became Catholic and also became part of Protestant religious movements. Serious genealogists with Huguenot ancestry should ask this question: were my ancestors Jews who joined with the Huguenots because they were an enemy of the Catholic Church? Jewish Huguenot

Pilgrims, who hid behind the veil of Protestant Christianity, were a stepping-stone away from Judaism, a religion of which many, probably most, did not return. Huguenot *and* Jewish communities backed up against each other in the north of France and Huguenots concentrated in the south and west of France as well, near Spain where Jews would have fled the Inquisition. It's an interesting question, what drove my ancestors from Catholic Europe to Protestant countries and the American Colonies?

I read an interesting book that spoke of the beginnings of the Ku Klux Klan. In this book, they stated that the KKK began after the Civil War, as a group of neighbors in the south, getting together to discuss rebuilding their communities. Can you imagine the stigma associated with having gone to a couple of these meetings? For those of us researching Southern roots, this is something we could run across. It is not easy for someone, whose ancestors held slaves, to go to an African-American ancestry board and post a message. But we can learn of our collective histories through our ancestor's relationships. You never know what you may find around the next corner. It is wonderful to see Southerners of both African-American and Caucasian ancestry collaborating on ancestry message boards. We have only begun.

I learned early, the importance and existence of cultures other than ours. My father was from New Orleans, one of the world's multi-cultural cities. He was vague about our ancestry. One day my sister asked me, "What are we?" Through the years my parents continued to enjoy a wide variety of cultures and during the 1960's began collecting antiques, especially antique clocks. One of their most treasured possessions was a rectangular, forest-green chandelier made with brass ornate trim. "It's Persian," my father would say while fingering it gently, "it's very valuable." While growing up in New Orleans, he was exposed to the history, culture and art of the French, Spanish, German, Portuguese, etc. Through my parent's antiques I learned about French cloisonné, early American tobacco humidors and Nefertiti from the antique pin my mother proudly displayed upon her clothes as if the beautiful Egyptian goddess was her token spirit and not only would she convey her beauty and power onto my mother, those who gazed at it would be transformed as well.

America's southern president, Bill Clinton has a nickname, "Bubba." It's a very popular southern pet name. I have a cousin in Louisiana we call "Bubbee." The word "Bubbee" is Yiddish, pronounced BUB-ee and is a "friendly term for anybody you like." Could this nickname have been a way for Southern Jews to retain *Jewish identity*? And similarly, South African Blacks known as *Lemba* have an oral history that they descend from the ancient Hebrews. They insist that they are Jewish. The elder clan member is called "Buba" which some say is the ancient name of the tribe's founder and that it means "from Judah." Those who have seen the *Lemba* say their skin color and facial structures are different from other Africans.

"Jews started trade routes between the islands and their mother countries. As we have seen, the Caribbean Jewish merchants were so successful that the other businessmen often persuaded their governments to tax or restrict Jewish trade. In spite of these attempts to put them out of business, Jewish communities flourished. In a time when the United States did not exist but was itself no more than a set of colonies, Jewish settlers looked to the religious and economic freedom they found in the New World to make new lives for themselves. We know Jews fleeing Brazil went to North American colonies as well as to the Caribbean. The Caribbean congregations helped support the Jewish communities that were starting in the United States. We know there was much travel and trade between the communities in the 'future' United States and the Caribbean. In fact, the Jews of the Caribbean are regarded, by many scholars, as the 'missing link' in the Jewish settlement of the early United States." Ralph G. Bennett - History of the Jews of the Caribbean

Jewish immigrants to North America wished to begin anew and wanted to partake of the same opportunities presented to all

48

immigrants. If they hadn't already, these Jewish immigrants either *Anglicized*, *Dutched up* or *Latinized* the sound and spelling of their names. Once this step was taken, it began a trek away from Judaism and the heritage they loved. For many, that was the last they saw of their Jewish roots. Once in the New World, their children were raised according to what was acceptable. When the Dutch were in control, it was the *Dutch Reformed Church*, when in French Louisiana territory it was *Catholicism*. That's why it's so shocking when coming from a family who practiced Christianity for centuries. It's hard to believe that an ancestor was Jewish if it was never spoken of, especially if our great-grandparents didn't even know. But the earliest ancestors knew and though they posed as Christians, they retained their cryptic communities and managed to have their children marry within their *Crypto-Jewish* group. Your Jewish ancestors may show up on church baptismal records but always remember, *the Inquisitions of Spain and Portugal and the persecution of Jews throughout Europe led to mass conversions.* For so many of our ancestors it was *do it or die,* period. So they did and here we are.

Galveston Texas was a port through which Jews came through when escaping the Russian army. I read one family historical account that stated that Jewish children were conscripted into the Russian army when they were as young as seven years old. Many modern day American Jews know they are Jewish but that's about it. After World War I, in some areas, there weren't that many Jews in America. Therefore, they had no one to teach them their religion and culture. A lot of the German Jews who "assimilated" denied they were Jews.

There were many instances of Early American French, Jewish, Dutch, English, etc. landowners taking African women as wives or concubines. Like many other ethnicities, the first Africans did not come to the colonies as slaves but came as Indentured Servants. Intermarriage with Native Americans between Africans was not uncommon as they found themselves in the same social strata, this occurred in Colonial Virginia. The Appalachian Mountain Portuguese also married Africans and Native Americans.

For us to find who our ancient ancestors were, we need to go back to the early days, way back. Back to Biblical days when Noah begat Ham who begat Cush who begat Seba. Noah's son Ham figures interestingly into the issue of ancient slavery. During the Middle Ages, both Christians and Muslims believed that the descendants of Ham had turned black because Ham's father, Noah, cursed him because Ham was drunk and naked. During the Middle Ages, Catholics and Calvinists believed it was this curse of Ham that made it acceptable to enslave people with black skin. We are grateful those eras are behind us.

Where am I going with all this? Quite simply, African Americans may find Jewish ancestry in their tree because many of the "New Christians" who were in Brazil and the Caribbean Islands were in the slave trading industry. These New Christians were formerly Jews. Please note that it is very offensive to Jews to imply that Jews were the major slave traders. This is not the case. The profiteering of human cargo took off like a firestorm across the developed world during the 1600's and 1700s, every ethnicity got in on it, including African Americans. But in his book, "The Slave Trade," author Hugh Thomas has gathered many names of Conversos (former Jews who converted to Christianity – *New Christians*) and their history including some of the locations where they conducted business. This can help African Americans AND Caucasians find their ancestry. How we connect to these hard to find ancestors is an incredible undertaking with much of it left to luck but I truly believe in Divine intervention and there is no better example of it then when one is researching ancestry as I'm sure many of you can attest.

"In Dutch Brazil, Jews flourished in the sugar industry, tax farming and slave trade. Jews often purchased slaves and resold them at great profit. Those they kept often preferred to work for Jews because both Shabbat and Sunday were rest days, whereas the Portuguese only gave them Sunday off, and the Dutch worked their slaves seven days a week."
Alden Oreck – The Virtual Jewish History Tour Brazil

The definition of a mausoleum is a "large and stately tomb." I had always heard about the cemetery where my grandparents were buried above ground as was traditional in New Orleans with its share of hurricanes and floods. If the caskets are not elevated ... well, there go the bodies. At the Hope Mausoleum in New Orleans, where my grandparents are buried we find a number of "clues." But let me reiterate, my grandparents did not maintain any resemblance of a Jewish identity. I had no idea what to expect but when my cousin's wife suspiciously said, "All the graves have these names, I think they're German." OK, interesting, especially since my grandparents were not German. The cemetery was very well kept, immaculate really. I did not have but an hour to visit but I jotted down many surnames then when I came home, I did some research:

Berckes is Hebrew and means "God is my judge" and it is from the Book of Daniel.
Glindmeyer in Hebrew means, "Who is like God."
Arndt was a "native of Berlin Germany," Arndt is a Jewish name.
Odendahl is a Jewish name.
Other names that could be Jewish: Moore, Scherr, Leonhardt, Thiemann, Glindmeyer (Glindmeir).

There were plenty of other names that I wrote down along with their German origins that were engraved upon their stones. There is a myriad of clues to follow. The sense that I came away with was that my Baptist ancestors, who are buried as either Wroten or Roten, were comfortable buried with people from Germany in a cemetery with few Christian crosses, at least in the section I visited. Whereas when I went to Acadiana, the cemetery I visited was very Latin and very Catholic, crosses and saints dominated. I left Hope Mausoleum feeling that there was a different "kind" of Crypto-Jew in Louisiana and the south, one of Ashkenazic origins. Are they the descendants of those who remember the "Black Code of Louisiana" of the late 1600's and early 1700's, where the first decree was "the expulsion of Jews from the colony"?

51

In 1724 the Governor of Louisiana, "Bienville" went about apprehending Jews as per the Black Code decree and because of this, on the north bank of the Ohio River, two or more Jewish traders were "burned at the stake" by the French. Although there was a three-month period in which the Jews were required to leave, many Jews were "rounded up" and marched to Fort Chartres across the Mississippi River into Illinois. My southern ancestors were around during this era. NO WONDER THEY KEPT QUIET. If you have ancestry who leave Louisiana around 1724 or who show up in Illinois at this time you might ask yourself why.

I recently read, that three-quarters of African-Americans' ancestors were in the colonies by 1776 and that in the 1870 census, it is unusual to find anyone born in Africa. African Americans have an extremely difficult time tracing their ancestry before the 1800s. But with the appreciation historians and genealogists have for collecting ship's records, finance sheets and records from households, I believe there is hope. I'm sure that an African American descendant of one whose life was stolen, would appreciate knowing from where their ancestor hailed. Many of these old records may help to reveal such origins in the coming years. Every day new records are scanned and put into the genealogical websites. There are fantastic websites springing up for African-Americans. Utilize them, the websites I viewed are run by scholars with devotion and determination. For more information on the topic of *Conversos, Marranos and Slave Traders* refer to my earlier book, **Secret Genealogy**. For extensive information, including maps, see *Slave Trade and African American Ancestry* - http://wysinger.homestead.com/mapofafricadiaspora.html

As I mentioned earlier, regarding *The Black Code*, King Louis of France, ruler of the Province and colony of Louisiana, in March of 1724, ordered, "all Jews who may have established their religion there be expelled within three months, under penalty of confiscation of body and property." Sounds like the Inquisition all over again. Here history shows the extension of persecution into the Southern New World. Not good for Jews hoping to practice their religion. Jews are given only three months before they start their round up of which the penalty is "confiscation of body and property." One need not leave that to the imagination, it is spelled out quite clearly. What would you do? What did our ancestors do? What choices did they have? They either left, again or did their best to remove any outward signs of Judaism lest they lose their land and maybe their life. And who has bigger mouths than little children? They would be foolish to practice Judaism in their homes or share it with the little ones, much as they would have loved. Thus began the death of their religion and probably their ethnicity. Here began the changing of names. In French Louisiana it was undoubtedly away from Hebrew and slanted toward sounding French, just as the Jews gave their children Dutch names to assimilate into New Amsterdam or Anglicized their surnames to assimilate into New York, although by the time of the English takeover, the English were better about their policies toward Jews. The big question is *what was their name before they assimilated?* You have to look at old records of names. Do you see similar names, do they sound similar? How would you change a Hebrew name to sound French, Dutch or English?

One of the definitions of **Creole** is a "person of mixed black and European, especially French or Spanish ancestry." There is a wonderful Cajun/Creole Cultural History Center in Acadiana in the city of Lafayette, Louisiana, called *Vermilionville.* Their mission is to keep the history and culture of Acadiana alive. If you are of African American Southern ancestry and you long for a trail to follow, you would enjoy visiting this center. The people in the gift shop, where you pay, are very friendly and helpful. They have reconstructed the lifestyles of the lives and culture of their southern Cajun and Creole ancestors in a respectful and charming way. On weekends they have get-togethers where they share in their culture with ethnic food and traditional music. There are lots of books to purchase and customs to explore. Even if you find no clues of your own, it is a delightful place that will stimulate your genealogical explorations.

I saw a posting on a genealogical message board that was very emphatic. *"I am waiting to discover that Cajuns are Jews,"* they write. *"The similarities are astonishing."* The cultural integration that has taken place in Acadiana, Louisiana attracts thousands of tourists each year. Members of this integration include descendants of African slaves who intermarried with Europeans, especially French and Spanish. But it is my belief that Jews who were hiding (or did not know of) their ethnicity were also integrated into this Acadian Louisiana cultural mix.

It's much harder to trace an ancestor when their surname is a common one. I spoke with a young African-American woman who can't trace very far back. She has the surname "Smith." Maybe the commonality of the name will work for her but trying to use a search engine with such a common name is asking for frustration frenzy. Better to hone in on some good family websites, keep impeccable records and stay focused, don't take too much time in-between search intervals, in other words ... don't let the trail grow cold.

If you think about it, Genealogy is like fortune telling except that it goes backwards into time. There is nothing like the excitement we experience when we open wide the lives of those who lived before us. Did their babies make it through the first year? Was anyone ever arrested or hung for treason? Did they save their land through the Great Panic or the Great Depression? And sometimes there are real doozies we find out about our ancestors; occasionally they do very human and sometimes bad things like abandon their families or take part in slave holding. Sometimes we find that they were the benefactors of others and kept it a secret, and sometimes we find that they kept their religion or ethnicity a secret. It's rather odd, this fascination we have over those who are no longer with us. But millions of people do and genealogy has become enormously popular. It is an addicting yet wonderful pastime watching your own novel unfold and it is a way in which we can leave a legacy for our descendants.

Chapter Eight

Conspiracy Theories

The Creation, Matthaeus Merian the Elder, 1625-30

It's interesting to think that when it was fashionable to worship "multiple" gods, it would be heresy to believe in the concept of "one" god. When studying the history of ancient mysteries, we are led to the Jews, monotheism, and ancient Masons who met in secret to share these mysteries. We read of Noah and his pure teachings. The word "Semite" derives from Noah's son Shem. In ancient times, a Semite was not chiefly represented by Jews and Arabs but included the Phoenicians, Assyrians, Babylonians, Aramaeans and others. Hidden within Secret Societies were our ancestors and their Secret Genealogy.

As descendants of Crypto-Jews we have many questions. Why does the family have so many secrets and what are the answers to those family secrets? Why was your family trying so hard to hide something and what was it? And one of my favorites, why oh why was your family hiding their real name? And why did they change it? Why did they hide the country that they originally came from? Why say you're from Holland (Italy, Portugal, or other) when you're not?

Why do the Dutch consider the Jews part of their heritage and America doesn't seem to embrace it? With all the colonial "Dutch" coming to America's shores shouldn't we see the Jews as more a part of our American heritage? Of course not, because they kept it hidden. America is full of these contradictions. If you read the ancestry message boards you'll see a lot of other folks "hid" too, the Irish, Scots-Irish, Native Americans, light-skinned African-Americans, everybody has their story. But one makes a great fool of himself in making inflammatory statements. Just as in political parties, there are both wonderful and despicable human beings in their ranks, so is it with the Jews as well as with Christians, Democrats, Republicans, Freemasons, Football players, actors, etc. There is a lot of rhetoric being bantered about. It makes it difficult to address accusations such as "The Jews are trying to take control of the world." The vast majority of the world's Jews are like the rest of us. Life is hard, especially in this new millennium and the Jews struggle just like the rest of us.

Spend a weekend thinking about all the groups who want to control the world. Be fair about it, take turns with each group and imagine all the ways they control your life, for instance: Environmentalists, Women, Men, The Church, Liberals, Conservatives, the list goes on. These groups are not the scourge of the earth because a few in their ranks have twisted minds. It seems to me, the person who gets caught up in the delusion that others are trying to control him or her has their own personal problems of feeling small in a world full of really bright people who are by nature ambitious and competitive. Last I noticed many groups were controlling my life. One would be wise to throw their support behind issues they find important. For me I value keeping our planet in tact, preserving nature and recognizing the relationship our survival has with nature's.

Spike Lee produced a movie called, "Inside Man." (Caution, spoiler alert). The story revolves around a man who is the CEO of the Board of Directors of a huge Manhattan bank. The CEO was a Jewish banker who betrayed his fellow Jews by selling out to the Nazis thereby amassing enormous wealth. In the movie, one of those hunting down the CEO was a Rabbi. Because there is "power in numbers" control of our world falls into the hands and minds of groups of people, any one can see that. And groups that have been disenfranchised, like minorities, have valid bitterness. Don't we tend to group with people who think like we do? And won't this probably go on forever? But when people speak of the danger of stereotyping, we should all take heed. To be prejudice is dangerous. Look how it has silenced our ancestors.

I run across a lot of inaccurate information about the Jews, much of it really hateful. Conspiracy theories regarding the Jews abound. True, there are bad Jews because there are bad everybody's, including bankers and yes there are plenty of Jews who are bankers because they became proficient money lenders due to their being excluded from trade guilds. History shows European rulers sometimes encouraged Jews to be moneylenders. But the Knights Templar are credited with establishing the world's first banking system and some believe the Knights Templar are the predecessors of today's Masons and our connection to the ancient Jews.

There are many origins of secret societies. I believe one of the origins of the group we have come to know as "Freemasons" began long ago when the Jews were displaced and scattered throughout the world. When skilled Jewish artisan craftsmen were captured as slaves, they fought as foot soldiers for the Roman army. Bravely they created their own "secret society" enabling them to continue with their promise to "help other Jews." For even in war, "brothers" could identify one another through secret handshakes, strange bird-like calls in the wilderness, expressions of speech and the leaving of their symbols carved upon elaborate stonework. Later, as freemen they continued to protect one another and pooled together to aid the widows of their brethren.

Modern Freemasons acknowledge that their organization has been around since before the Middle Ages, yet no records were kept. The first British initiation ceremony was in May of 1641. Yet the brotherhood of "Comacini Masons," centered in Lombardy during the early Middle Ages, have their first mention in 643 when King Rothari (a Lombard although Roth is a Jewish surname) discusses liability issues surrounding a construction project. The sculptural work of the "Como-Pavian" brotherhood of masons is found in England, Italy, France, Hungary, Germany, the Iberian Peninsula, Syria and Sweden. Like all artists, the Comacini Masons probably borrowed from other craftsmen and others undoubtedly borrowed from them. Throughout the world you will see the influence of these highly skilled masons, especially in Europe when greeted by gargoyles. African, Gothic, Asian, Hebraic and Arabic patterns and geometrical designs that we see throughout the world influenced the Comacini Masons as well.

Words like mysteries, craft, masters, secret, cryptic, etc. lead to the mysticism surrounding the legends of the men and women of secret societies. How can we not be mystified by men who were captured by the Romans, made slaves, turned into soldiers and took it upon themselves to create secret organizations in order to care for their loved ones in the event they died in battle? Secret Societies house museums of their regalia of foreign wars. This can be confusing but if you were to think of them as members of an elite group, often on opposing sides, it is more understandable. The truth is, Jews took seriously their vows to watch and care for other Jews. There is an ancient phrase *Kol Yisrael arevim zeh la-zeh*, which translated means "all the people of Israel are responsible for one another."

"The great central fact about the Roman civilization is that by their earlier conquests they had inherited the wisdom of the ancient Near East, Egypt and Babylonia, the Israelites and Assyrians, the Minoans, Mycenaeans, and Achaeans; the Medes and Persians had all in their time contributed to a civilization which made its supreme bid for power, and met its defeat at the hands of the Greeks at Salamis in 480 B.C."
EVERYDAY LIFE IN ROMAN AND ANGLO-SAXON TIMES, by Marjorie and C.H.B. Quennell, Dorset Press, 1987.

Napoleon recognized the Jews took their vow to be responsible for one another seriously and that they were fiercely independent. He said the Jews were "a nation within a nation." In 1806 Napoleon ordered 45 rabbis and 26 laymen to form the *Grand Sanhedrin*. The *Grand Sanhedrin* was a Jewish high court system under the control of the Napoleonic government, meant to override the ancient Jewish court system called the *Sanhedrin*.

"Brussels Lion"

"There is some probability that Jews in small numbers were settled in England at an early date. They were the property and protégés of the crown, being used because, while the Church prohibited loans on interest, and the medieval states could not exist without such loans, Jews were permitted and encouraged to act as financial capitalists. Before the age of Titus, as Josephus informs us, the Jews were a non-commercial people. It was a result of their divorce from their old agricultural life that forced them into trade." GROLIER ENCYCLOPEDIA VOL 11 & 12, p. 268, THE GROLIER SOCIETY, INC, 1956, USA

Chapter Nine

Aryans, Arians, Anglos, Saxons and Jutes

The Anglos

The "Angles" were Low German tribes who with the Saxons and Jutes conquered England in the 5th century A.D. From the Angles come the words English, England and Anglian. Could any of the "Anglos" who conquered England in the 5th century, been Jewish tribes?

This was and is a strange puzzle that began with a Jewish friend's genealogy. Both of his parents are Jewish and it is believed their surname "Galerkin" was brought to Russia from Greece hundreds of years ago. Let's separate the name, Galer kin. Kin of Galer? Although this is a Jewish name, it sounds like it could have been Gaelic-kin.

Gael – n. A Gaelic-speaking Celt of Scotland, Ireland, or the Isle of Man.

I'm wondering if the Jews were not interspersed with Celtic tribes who migrated into England from Gaul (France). Gaul-erkin? The Jews have had a presence in Britain for over a thousand years perhaps much longer. The Galerkins are Jewish, we are not trying to prove that. I'm just wondering if the Galerkins are the descendants of Jews who migrated through France into England and lived in Britain as early agriculturalists.

"Ingles" is another surname in the Galerkin family. Their oral history is that Ingles is the "Hebrew-Yiddish-German word for angel." "Ingle" is a Scottish word, probably French Gael, meaning fire so that fits with my hearing "Gaelic-kin" in Galerkin even though Galerkin and Ingles are two different surnames among many in this family tree. But they were told that "Ingles" means "angel." The name *Aingeal* is a variant of the Greek Angela and the meaning is "messenger of God," sounds like an angel yet it also comes so near the sound of "Angles" from whence came the words *England* and *English*. *Angli* is French Teutonic.

But the Galerkins are wrong about Ingles being Yiddish for angel. Yahoo.com has this answer: *"An angel is a 'Malech' in Yiddish. It is actually said the same way in Hebrew."* One thing I've found in doing years of genealogical research is NEVER toss oral history aside; it is always connected in one way or another. Further searching started showing Spanish associations and then I remembered Ingles is Spanish for "English" giving us images of England, early Celts, Gauls and Spain. I looked up "Ingles" at sephardim.com and found it listed in the "Dictionary of Sephardic Surnames," listed as "immigrants to Brazil."

We know that the Galerkin oral history mentions Greece as the oldest location the family had knowledge of. *Anglo-Saxones* is the Middle Latin term for a *"member of the nation created by the consolidation of Low German tribes that invaded England in the 5th and 6th centuries, together with native and Danish elements..."*

Another definition of Anglo-Saxon is a *"member of, or a descendant from the mixed race which forms the English nation."* I had mentioned earlier that the Jews had a historical presence in England for a thousand years, perhaps longer and this definition states *"mixed race."*

Ancestry searching takes us to places we never imagined. Lots of surprises, which is why people love it. There are those who say the English were one of the lost tribes of Israel. With all the researching I do, one commonality is that "tribes" ventured from Mediterranean locales and fanned out in all directions.

The Aryans

The Aryans used the swastika as a sun symbol; the Nazis used it as an icon. But long before that, the swastika was incorporated into early Christian art. The Sanskrit meaning of it is "well-being." The word Aryan conjures up images of Hitler. For the Nazis, Aryan meant *"Caucasians who weren't Jews."*

Who the Aryans are has always baffled me. Hitler believed that the Aryan Race was a "pure" Germanic race, which he meant to preserve. Then I heard that Iran means Aryan because *they* were Aryans. My search for finding *exactly* who the Aryans are (or were) has brought me this:

Aryans descended on the river valleys of northern India around 2000 BC.
Aryans are light-skinned and probably came from Central Asia or Europe.
Aryans are of the same stock as Europeans.
Aryans were warriors on chariots.
Hinduism stemmed from ancient Aryans and their writings; they are credited with writing mankind's oldest book 'the Vedas'.

If I go by what my newer dictionary defines, it would tell me the root of the word *arya* means noble, but other than that it just tells me that an Aryan is a descendant of prehistoric people who spoke Indo-European. And for the second definition it states Indo-Iranian. Still not enough information for my brain to form a concise picture of who the Aryans are (or were). I have an old 1941 dictionary, which describes it further, by informing me that, the Aryans descend from the Iranian plateau from ancient times while another branch entered India. One thing I'm sure of is that they are Caucasian.

Now we tackle the difference between Arian and Aryan. These words have different meanings. Arianism is the belief that Jesus was special but not the eternal Son of God, nor the same substance as God. Hitler custom designed his own Arian beliefs based on the ancient *doctrines of Arius*. So it makes it confusing that Hitler was both an *Arian* and an *Aryan*.

The Saxons

Saxon is an old French word of which the plural is *Saxones*. The Saxones were of ancient Germanic origin who with the Jutes conquered and colonized England. One of the definitions of "Anglo-Saxon" is quite simply *Old English*. The Teutonic (ancient Germanic) tribes include: Burgundians, Goths, Franks, Vandals, Lombards, Angles, Saxons, Jutes, Danes and Norwegians. Pretty wide group of folks.

Elizabeth Caldwell Hirschman and Donald N. Yates have written a book, *When Scotland Was Jewish*. Their book states that "the ancestors of these persons originated in France and Spain and then made their way to Scotland's shores, moors, burgs and castles from the reign of Malcolm Canmore to the aftermath of the Spanish Inquisition."

If these authors are correct, one could surmise that the Jews who were "Old English" could have settled in England while others moved on to Scotland or Ireland. I have ancestry with the surname "Holmes" which I felt, in no way were they Jewish but probably English or especially Irish as they descend from Ireland but when I went to Israel there was this huge store with the name Holmes big and bold. Made me laugh. Not that they were necessarily Jewish but I was no longer positive they weren't.

The Jews have been in Germany for well over a thousand years. Although Jewish religious custom was to marry within their tribe, we know that those rules were broken. Another one of the dictionary's definitions of Teutonic is *"designating or pertaining to, the tall blond race characteristic of northern Europe."* The fact that there are blonde Jews attests to these rules being broken. Yes, the Jews stuck together and married within, but history constantly reminds us what happens during warfare and love. How many fairy tales are based on love between two members of opposing groups? For some of us, this is how Jewish ancestry entered into our family tree. For most of us, I suspect our Jewish ancestors, unfortunately, sort of faded into the background of history. Not that they wanted to. But the fact that we can find them today tells us that their intent was not to sever that bridge entirely, just close it for a while. For our families, we do what we have to do; the rest is left to fate.

The Jutes

The Jutes were members of one of the Low German tribes of Jutland, some of them settled in Kent, England after their 5th century invasion. An adjective for Jute is "Jutish" pronounced *jootish*. I can hear a Danish-accented tongue saying *Jute* for Judah. Judah of course, meaning the *tribe of Judah*. Listen to the sounds ... Tribe of *Judah* ... Tribe of *Jute* ... but that would be silly to assume from that alone. But, Jews from Germany are Germans as well as Jews, so why not *Jutes?*

Christian IV was the first Danish king to establish connections with Jews but the years mentioned are 1588-1648, we are researching much earlier, the 5th century. But ... a popular variety of "jute" is mentioned in *The Book of Job* in the Hebrew Bible, calling the herb *jute*, "Jew's mallow." Co-incidence? Another interesting fact is that the Jutes' pottery and jewelry is different from Anglo and Saxon pottery and jewelry. Another way in which the Jutes differed from the Anglicans and the Saxons was their burial practice. Cremation was popular with the Anglos and Saxons, and it was practiced longer with the Anglos. But burial in the ground was the favorite of the Jutes as is the case for the Jews.

Besides being a tribe and twine, Jute is a Bengali and French Sanskrit word for "matted hair." Let's separate Bengali ... Ben Gali. Ben means son so could Bengali mean *son of the Gauls?* The name "Gali Baba" represents Sephardic Jewish immigrants to Brazil, as does the name "Ben Galil." My understanding is that Bengal refers to people as in *the Bengali people*.

There is a lot of controversy and scholarly arguments about whether or not the Anglos, Saxons, and Jutes are from the lost tribes of Israel. Some researchers insist that British means "Covenant Man" in Hebrew. I do not know if we have made a connection through the Galerkin's "Ingles" but it underscores how important everyone's genealogical record is and how one minor detail can have a dramatic impact. Can you imagine how elated one would feel when finding that their surname was a missing link between the ancient Israelites and the Anglos?"

During the Anglo-Saxon, Viking and Norman eras in England, I found some interesting names:
617 AD Eadwine, King of Northumbria. *d.* 633
899 AD EADWARD THE ELDER. *d.* 924
I find this interesting because Edward is a popular Jewish name and there are many during this era, lots of Eadward, Eadred, Eadgar, Eadmund, etc.
But even more intriguing is this:
796 AD Coenwulf, King of Mercia. *d.* 821
Coen? Can you get a more Jewish name than that?

An English history book, WROUGHTON THROUGH THE MISTS OF TIME, attempts to simplify things: "Anglo-Saxon became the overall term for the ruling classes and eventually English became both the name for the people of most of Britain and for the language spoken by them." That said, it is still confusing. After the Romans left what is now England, British became the name used for the natives that remained and Anglo-Saxon was a "collective" term used for the Angles, Saxons and Jutes who populated the area later. Celtic identified the "purer strains of the earlier race, particularly in the far west..." "Romano-British is the title given to the descendants of the Celts, Romans and North European soldiers and traders."

Interesting Websites

The Association of Crypto Jews
http://www.cryptojew.org/main_page.html

The Twelve Tribes of Israel Engraved Upon Stone
http://www.templesanjose.org/JudaismInfo/history/12tribes.htm

A Resource for Turkic and Jewish History in Russia and Ukraine
http://www.khazaria.com/

United States Holocaust Memorial Museum
http://www.ushmm.org/research/collections/

Online Jewish Encyclopedia
http://www.jewishencyclopedia.com/

Jewish Symbolism
http://www.mechon-mamre.org/jewfaq/signs.htm

Jewish Names
http://www.behindthename.com/names/usage/jewish

History of Jewish Working Lives
http://www.movinghere.org.uk/galleries/histories/jewish/working_lives/working_lives.htm

Distribution of Blood Types by Dennis O'Neil
http://anthro.palomar.edu/vary/vary_3.htm

PolandGenWeb - Help Pages - Regions of Poland - Past and Present
http://www.rootsweb.ancestry.com/~polwgw/areas.html

Jewish Web Index
http://jewishwebindex.com/France.htm

Judaism 101
http://www.jewfaq.org/torah.htm

Lost Israelite Identity, The Hebrew Origin of Celtic Races"
http://britam.org/dan.html

Israelites Came to Ancient Japan
http://www5.ocn.ne.jp/~magi9/isracame.htm

Hebrew for Christians
http://www.hebrew4christians.com/Glossary/Yiddish_Words/yiddish_words.html
(You could find a surname in their glossary of Yiddish words and phrases.)

Rabbi Yaakov Kleiman
TRIBES OF ISRAEL LOST & FOUND / ANCIENT & MODERN
http://www.cohen-levi.org/the_tribe/tribes_of_israel.htm

University of Notre Dame Latin Dictionary and Grammar Aid
http://archives.nd.edu/latgramm.htm

This is the list of names of the Portuguese Sephardim who were paid to leave Amsterdam during the years 1757 - 1813
http://www.saudades.org/leaveamsterdam.html

Notarial Records from Amsterdam's Portuguese Jewish Community that Mention Danzig
http://www.jewishgen.org/Danzig/amsterdam.php

Shira Schoenberg's Virtual Jewish History Tour of England
http://www.jewishvirtuallibrary.org/jsource/vjw/England.html

Comacine masters
http://en.wikipedia.org/wiki/Comacine_masters

An Index to the Given Names in the 1292 Census of Paris
http://heraldry.sca.org/laurel/names/paris.html

This is an excellent website for researching Dutch History
http://www.rabbel.nl/oldplaces1.html

Netherlands Society for Jewish Genealogy
http://www.nljewgen.org/eng/index.html

Jewish Genealogy/Dutch
http://www.dutchjewry.org/

Sephardic Surnames from a number of Jewish Sephardic sources
http://www.sephardicgen.com/names.htm

Search for ancestors among free lists and records
http://www.olivetreegenealogy.com/nn/

Cyndi's List of Genealogy Sites on the Internet
http://www.cyndislist.com

Cyndi's List/Jewish
http://www.CyndisList.com/jewish.htm

Istanbul Jewish Genealogy Project (almost 100,000 records)
http://www.benkazez.com/dan/istanbul/

Definitions of the world's major religions and belief systems
http://www.cftech.com/BrainBank/OTHERREFERENCE/RELIGI
ON/MajorReligion.html

Avotaynu: Resources for tracing Jewish Family History
www.avotaynu.com/nu.htm

For a study on hypocorism (a naming pattern)
http://en.wikipedia.org/wiki/Hypocorism

Jewish Names and Naming Patterns
https://wiki.familysearch.org/en/Jewish_Names_Personal

A List of Jewish Surnames, History and Origin
http://humora.tripod.com/Surnames.html

Southern Appalachian / Melungeon Heritage
http://www.melungeon.org/

An interesting discussion about similarities between Cajuns and Jews
http://www.freerepublic.com/focus/f-news/1337161/replies?c=25

Behind the Name/the etymology and history of first names
www.behindthename.com

History of the Oddfellows
http://www.oddfellows.org.uk/History.htm

An Interesting and Historically Informative Article Regarding Maranos
http://www.jewishencyclopedia.com/view.jsp?artid=169&letter=M

A short history of the famous scholar and orator, Menasseh Ben Israel, beloved by both Jews and Gentiles
http://www.saudades.org/menasseh.html

Glossary

Acadia – original French name of Nova Scotia

Acadian – from Acadia (descendants of African slaves who intermarried with Europeans, especially French and Spanish)

Acadiana - culturally rich region in Louisiana, home of the descendants of the Acadians

Akkad – (Accad) the northern division of ancient Babylonia

Akkadian – one of the Semitic people of Mesopotamia before 2000 B.C.E.

Anglicize – to translate, reword or express into English usage

Anglo-Saxon – a member of the nation created by the merger of Germanic tribes who invaded England and resided from the fifth to the eleventh centuries; person of English descent consisting of mixed races; "Old English"

Anusim - an ancient Hebrew word meaning "people who have been forced"

Arab – member of a Semitic race from the Arabian Peninsula and North Africa

Ashkenazi – noun for a Yiddish-speaking Jew from Middle, Northern and Eastern Europe (Ashkenazim is plural whereas Ashkenazic is used as the adjective)

Auto de Fe - the Inquisitional ceremony that pronounced the judgment of execution, which usually meant burning heretics to death

Bani-Israel - Children of Israel

Beni-Israel - Jews who settled in Bombay, India beginning in the 12th century. Today they are Muslim, living in Pakistan and Afghanistan

Bible – sacred book of Christians (Old & New Testaments); sacred book of Judaism (Old Testament), referred to as the Torah

Black Dutch – a term sometimes used by Native Americans to conceal their ethnicity (also Black Irish); a term sometimes used by the Dutch for the Spanish Jews who immigrated to the Netherlands in the 16th century; a term sometimes used by German Jews to conceal their ethnicity

Cajun – person of Acadian descent

Calque – used in Jewish naming patterns, the process of taking a word from the local language that's similar to the sacred name and using it for a name (a translation)

Celt - One of an ancient people of West and Central Europe, including the Britons and the Gauls

Celtic - A group of Indo-European languages, including Welsh and Gaelic

Christian – believer in Christianity; member of a Christian church; person whose life and character conform to Christ's teachings

Christianize – to make Christian; to convert to Christianity

Christian name – first name, given to Christians at baptism

Cochin - Ancient Jews of India's Malabar Coast, "Malabar Yehudan"

Converso – a Jew who converted to Christianity, usually by force or coercion

Court Jews (Hofjude) - Jews attaining powerful positions in European aristocracy as bankers, money managers, consultants, trade and political representatives, etc.

Crypto Jew – practicing Judaism in secret while professing another religious faith

Diaspora – Jews scattered throughout the ancient world after Exile

Emigrate – to leave a country or region to settle in another

Eponym – historical or legendary person from whom a family, nation, race, etc. takes its name

Gael – n. a Gaelic-speaking Celt of Scotland, Ireland, or the Isle of Man

Gaelic – n. a branch of the Celtic languages – Gaelic – adj

Hasidim – meaning "the pious," a Jewish religious movement that began in the 1700s, focusing on the emotions and sentiments of faith rather than dogma and ritual

Hassidic - of or relating to the Jewish Hasidim or its members or their beliefs and practices

Hebraic - of or pertaining to the Hebrews or to the Hebrew kingdom in Southern Palestine

Hebrew – member of one of the Semitic peoples inhabiting ancient Palestine; language of the Hebrews; also a book in the New Testament of the Bible

Hebrew-Christian - A Christian of Jewish ethnicity

<u>Hellenist</u> - one who affiliates with Greeks, or imitates Greek manners; esp., a Jew who used the Greek language as his mother tongue."

<u>Heretic</u> – one who holds an opinion contrary to Christian belief and encourages separation from the church

<u>Hittite</u> - ancient people who invaded and conquered Asia Minor and Syria 2000 B.C.E., possibly of Ancient Germanic origin

<u>Huguenot</u> – a French Protestant during the 16th & 17th centuries (Walloon refers to Belgian Protestants)

<u>Hypocorism</u> – a hypocorism is the lesser form of a given name used in more intimate situations, like a nickname, originating from the Greek expression to "use child talk"

<u>Immigrate</u> - to come into a country as a permanent resident

<u>Indentured Servants</u> – apprentice bound to a master by a contract, or to service in a colony etc.

<u>Inquisition</u> – the establishment of the Holy Office (tribunal) used to pursue and punish heretics

<u>Israel</u> – used to describe: the northern Hebrew kingdom, the descendants of Jacob (Jews) and/or the republic in SW Asia along the Mediterranean

<u>Jew</u> – a member of the ancient tribe of Judah, also, one who practices the religion of Judaism, a Hebrew

<u>Jewish</u> – pertinent to or like the Jews

<u>Judah</u> – son of Jacob and Leah, also; one of the twelve tribes of Israel, also; the Hebrew kingdom in Southern Palestine

<u>Judaism</u> – religion, culture and ethos of the Jews

<u>Judaize</u> – to conform, or to convert, to the doctrines, observances, or methods of the Jews

<u>Judea</u> – the southern area of ancient Palestine that formed the kingdom of the tribes of Judah and Benjamin

<u>Khazars</u> - ancient Eastern European Jews

<u>Kinnui</u> – (kinouy, kinui) not a sacred Jewish name but a name that relates to the immediate environment, a secular name required at circumcision along with the sacred name

<u>Kosher</u> – (kasher) from the Hebrew word meaning "fit" or "proper," usually used to define food that has been ritually cleaned according to Jewish law

Ladino – the mixed Spanish and Hebrew language spoken by Sephardim

Law of the Pure Blood – a prohibition against migrating to Mexico unless one could prove that the last three generations of their family had been "Old Christians"

Marrano – taken from the Spanish word "swine," it was used for Jews who professed Christianity only to escape death or persecution during the Inquisition, while often continuing to observe Judaism secretly. It is believed the term came about when Jews broke kosher dietary laws and put pork in their food to prove they no longer practiced Judaism

Matronymic – name derived from that of the mother

Medieval – of or pertaining to the Middle Ages

Melungeon – a group of people descended from European and Middle Eastern ancestry who intermarried with Native Americans and African Americans and reside along North America's Atlantic coast, including northeastern Tennessee and southwestern Virginia

Mexican Inquisition – an extension of the Spanish Inquisition into the New World

Misyavnim - name Jews gave themselves in 200 B.C.E. when they abandoned their culture and embraced Greek culture, meaning "Hellenists"

Mizrahi Jews - the Jews of Babylon and Persia

Moor – native of Morocco or North African states; a Moslem or Arab who settled in North Africa; a descendant of the Saracens who invaded Spain during the Middle Ages

Morisco – a Moor, especially of Spain

Mulatto – person with a light-browned skin pigmentation of mixed African and Caucasian ancestry

New Christian – Jews or Moors who converted or were forced to convert to Christianity during the Middle Age's Inquisitional period

Patronymic – name derived from that of the father

Pentateuch - the first five books of the Old Testament, collectively

Portuguese Merchants - prominent Crypto-Jews having extensive commercial networking capabilities who fled to Holland during Spain and Portugal's Inquisitions

<u>Pureza de la sangre</u> – "purity of the blood" certificate needed during the Mexican Inquisition to avoid arrest

<u>Rabbi</u> – spiritual leader of a Jewish synagogue; a Jewish teacher or doctor of the law

<u>Sabbatarian</u> - one who believes the fourth commandment requires keeping the seventh day of the week holy

<u>Samaria</u> – ancient region of Palestine

<u>Samaritan</u> - a native or inhabitant of ancient Samaria closely related to Jews *and* Gentiles

<u>Saracen</u> - a term for an Arab or Moslem during the Middle Ages especially, one who expressed opposition to the Christian Crusades

<u>Schem Hakodesch</u> – sacred Hebrew name required at circumcision, the name is used in Hebrew documents and in the synagogue

<u>Semite</u> – a descendant of Shem (a son of Noah); a member of a Caucasian race now chiefly represented by the Jews and Arabs, but in ancient times included the Phoenicians, Assyrians, Babylonians, Aramaeans, etc

<u>Semitic</u> – of or pertinent to the Semites

<u>Sephardim</u> – descendants of the former Jews of Spain and Portugal (Sephardim is the noun, Sephardic is the adjective)

<u>Slave</u> – a person held in bondage

<u>Synagogue</u> – Jewish house of worship

<u>Tanakh</u> - same books of the Bible as in the Old Testament but not in the same order

<u>Torah</u> – entire body of Jewish law, the *Pentateuch,* which is the first five books of the Old Testament of the Bible

<u>Walloon</u> – a term used to refer to Belgian Protestants, while the term "Huguenot" denotes French back-ground

<u>Yiddish</u> – a High German dialect developed under Hebrew and Slavic influence, written in Hebrew letters

<u>Voorleser</u> – the Dutch word for an educated man who read lessons in church (absent a pastor) led singing, taught school and performed other duties

Bibliography

Photo on title page: Jews praying in the Synagogue on Yom Kippur. (1878 painting by Maurycy Gottlieb)

A WORK OF COMPASSION? Dutch slavery and slave trade in the Indian Ocean in the seventeenth century, by Markus P. M. Vink, SUNY-College at Fredonia.
http://www.historycooperative.org/proceedings/seascapes/vink.html

Baltic States and Central Europe, Lands and Peoples, VOLUME V, THE GROLIER SOCIETY INC., New York, 1956.

Columbus (Ohio) Jewish Historical Society
http://www.columbusjewishhistory.org/ojc.html

EVERYDAY LIFE IN ROMAN AND ANGLO-SAXON TIMES, by Marjorie and C.H.B. Quennell, Dorset Press, 1987.

Hebrew For Christians/Yiddish Words
http://www.hebrew4christians.com/Glossary/Yiddish_Words/yiddish_words.html

Jewishhistory.org
http://www.jewishhistory.org/the-hell-in-hellenism/

Origins and Diversity of the Taiwanese People
http://www.taiwandna.com/JewishPage.htm

Rembrandt's Jews, by Steven Nadler, The University of Chicago Press, Chicago, 2003.

Sephardim.com, an excellent resource for searching Sephardic surnames
www.sephardim.com

THE GIFTS OF THE JEWS, How a Tribe of Desert Nomads Changed the Way Everyone Thinks and Feels, by Thomas Cahill, Nan A. Talese, Bantam Doubleday Dell, NY, 1998.

The Hittites, People of a Thousand Gods, by Johannes Lehmann, Translated by J. Maxwell Brownjohn, The Viking Press, New York, NY, 1977.

THE HOLY BIBLE, ENCYCLOPEDIC INDEX, CONCORDANCE AND DICTIONARY, CONSOLIDATED BOOK PUBLISHERS, CHICAGO, ILLINOIS, 1956.

The Influence of Sephardic Jews and Moors on Southeastern Indian Cultures, by Donald Panther-Yates
http://www.jewishindy.com/modules.php?name=News&file=articl e&sid=8268

The Jerusalem Post
http://www.jpost.com/Opinion/Columnists/Article.aspx?id=23797 7

The Lost Years of Jesus Revealed, by the Rev. Dr. Charles Francis Potter, Fawcett Publications, Inc., USA, 1958.

The Scribner-Bantam English Dictionary, Bantam Books, NY, NY, 1980.

The Slave Trade, by Hugh Thomas, Simon & Schuster, New York, NY, 1997.

Three Baltic Countries: Esthonia, Latvia and Lithuania, Grolier Encyclopedia, Lands & Peoples, Vol II p. 173, NY, 1956.

Was Israel Ever in Egypt? Or, a Lost Tradition?, by George Henry Bateson Wright, Williams and Norgate,1895.

Sample
Secret Genealogy III
From Jewish-Anglo-Saxon Tribes to New France Acadians
by
Suellen Ocean

Chapter One

Gathering the Truth

I started writing my first *Secret Genealogy* book about 2007 when Crypto-Jewish discussions on the Internet were rare. Few authors were willing to look like fools and state that Americans have unclaimed Jewish ancestry. Crypto-Jews had been discussed in regard to Europe, Africa and the Middle East but not usually America because it was believed the majority of American Jews didn't show up until the 1800's. It was a bit of a stretch to include them in early Colonial history.

There are numerous Crypto-Jewish organizations and the number of books on the subject, particularly those centering on America's Southwest, has grown substantially. Professor Lavendar at Florida International University has been lecturing for years about the possibility of Jews posing as Huguenots and because of the growth of ancestry.com and research by authors like Donald Panther-Yates and Elizabeth Caldwell Hirschman, more people are discovering Jewish ancestry. The authors who suggest that Anglo-Americans can have Jewish ancestry have gained an audience.

Knowing who my ancestors were and how they evolved into their American identity helps me to know who *I* am. I find it interesting that the religious nature of my parents and grandparents might not stem from their Christianity, but because their ancient ancestors had been religious Jews. I did not write this book because of any religious agenda that I have. Although I have strong spiritual beliefs, I have not been affiliated with any religious groups since I was a child. I rather enjoy sitting back and listening, taking it all in. Religion is fascinating and can be colorful and culturally awakening. But we all know how destructive religion has been throughout world history. My hope is that *people of all creeds* will feel welcome to use my *Secret Genealogy* books to understand the history of the evolution of Hebrew-Christians and as a guide to their own genealogy.

Secret Genealogy III available here:
http://www.amazon.com/Secret-Genealogy-III-Jewish-Anglo-Saxon-Acadians/dp/148407579X

www.ingramcontent.com/pod-product-compliance
Lightning Source LLC
Chambersburg PA
CBHW070559290526
45790CB00002B/733